THE PORCUPINE

is

'superbly accomplished' *Sunday Times*
'vivid and compelling' *Allan Massie*
'a masterpiece' *Robert Harris*

John Bayley has praised its mesmeric charm,
Caroline Moore its clarity,
elegance and humane intelligence

JULIAN BARNES

Read it and decide for yourself
THE TRUTH CAN BE SHARPER IN FICTION
Jonathan Cape £9.99

New American fiction available in *flamingo* **O**RIGINAL *paperback*

AGNES ROSSI
THE QUICK
A NOVELLA AND
STORIES

3 DECEMBER

'The Quick *attests to the emergence of a richly gifted writer, a dazzling ventriloquist*'
NEW YORK TIMES

DOROTHY ALLISON
BASTARD OUT OF
CAROLINA

7 JANUARY

'*Resonant, emotionally complex, and strong as hell*'
MARY GAITSKILL, *author of BAD BEHAVIOR and TWO GIRLS, FAT AND THIN*

ROBERT O'CONNOR
BUFFALO SOLDIERS

25 FEBRUARY

'Buffalo Soldiers *is an M-1 tank of a novel, fast and powerful and dangerous*'
JAY McINERNEY

ALSO AVAILABLE IN
FLAMINGO PAPERBACK

FROM THE AUTHOR OF
RICH IN LOVE
NOW A MAJOR FILM
STARRING ALBERT FINNEY

JOSEPHINE HUMPHREYS
THE FIREMAN'S FAIR

3 DECEMBER

'*Warm, whimsical and wise*'
RUTH RENDELL

 An imprint of HarperCollins*Publishers*

GRANTA

KRAUTS!

42

Editor: Bill Buford
Deputy Editor: Tim Adams
Managing Editor: Ursula Doyle
Editorial Assistant: Cressida Leyshon
Contributing Editor: Rose Kernochan

Managing Director: Catherine Eccles
Financial Controller: Geoffrey Gordon
Circulation Manager: Sally Lewis
Subscriptions Assistant: Deanna Holmes
Office Assistant: Edward MacDermott

Picture Editor: Alice Rose George
Design: Chris Hyde
Executive Editor: Pete de Bolla
US Publisher: Anne Kinard, Granta, 250 West 57th Street, Suite 1316, New York, NY 10107.

Editorial and Subscription Correspondence: Granta, 2–3 Hanover Yard, Noel Road, Islington, London N1 8BE. Telephone: (071) 704 9776. Fax: (071) 704 0474. Subscriptions: (071) 704 0470.
A one-year subscription (four issues) is £21.95 in Britain, £25.95 for the rest of Europe, and £31.95 for the rest of the world.
All manuscripts are welcome but must be accompanied by a stamped, self-addressed envelope or they cannot be returned.

Granta is printed in the United States of America. The paper used in this publication meets the minimum requirements of American National Standard for Information Sciences—Permanence of Paper for Printed Library Materials, ANSI Z39.48-1984 ∞

Granta is published by Granta Publications Ltd and distributed by Penguin Books Ltd, Harmondsworth, Middlesex, England; Viking Penguin, a division of Penguin Books USA Inc, 375 Hudson Street, New York, NY 10014, USA; Penguin Books Australia Ltd, Ringwood, Victoria, Australia; Penguin Books Canada Ltd, 2801 John Street, Markham, Ontario, Canada L3R 1BR; Penguin Books (NZ) Ltd, 182–190 Wairau Road, Auckland 10, New Zealand. This selection copyright © 1992 by Granta Publications Ltd.

Cover by Senate.
Cover photo by Anthony Binder (Network). Inset photo by Holger Flob (Network).

Granta 42, Winter 1992
ISBN 0140 140 530

ADULT *Images*

Adult Comics

An Introduction

Roger Sabin

The first survey of comic books for older readers from the end of the 19th Century to the present – taking in pre-Great War titles, the underground of the 1960s, fandom in the 70s and 80s and today's boom including 'graphic novels' and *Viz.*

New Accents

March 1993: 234x156: 256pp
Hb: £35.00 Pb: £9.99

Arresting Images

Impolitic and Uncivil Actions

Steven C. Dubin

'With exemplary clarity and insight, Steven Dubin assesses the growing maelstrom over 'correct' art, censored art and contentious art. Essential reading for anyone interested in these debates and controversies.' – *Judith R. Blau, University of North Carolina*

March 1993: 216x138: 368pp
illus. 25 b&w and 2 colour plates Hb: £19.99

The Female Nude

Art, Obscenity and Sexuality

Lynda Nead

Lynda Nead presents the first feminist survey of the most significant subject in Western art. She reveals how the female nude is now both at the centre and at the margins of high culture.

December 1992: 234x156: 240pp
illus. 40 b&w photographs Hb: £35.00 Pb: £10.99

J. Arthur Rank and the British Film Industry

Geoffrey MacNab

Combining archival research with interviews with Rank's contemporaries and family, this definitive study charts every aspect of the 1940's "golden era" of the British film industry that Rank helped to create.

Cinema and Society

April 1993: 234x156: 320pp
illus. 36 plates Hb: £30.00

Available through booksellers.
For more information please contact:
James Powell, Routledge, 11 New Fetter Lane,
London EC4P 4EE

ROUTLEDGE

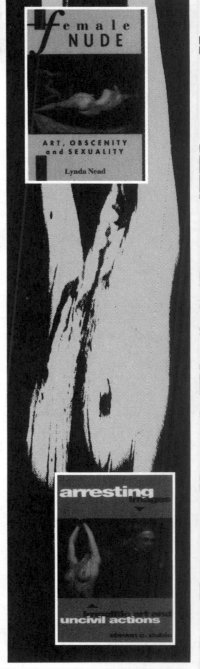

Contents

Eve's Tattoo **Emily Prager**
'A book that glitters with black mischief, is grue-
somely funny and brilliantly written' *Sunday Times*

Judge on Trial **Ivan Klima**
'A great novel which transmits in detail the
special qualities of life in a nightmare' *Independent*

Distant Voices **John Pilger**
'A brave and invaluable witness to his time'
Martha Gellhorn

The Journals **John Cheever**
'He wrote like an angel and his journals could
easily prove as addictive as gin' *Daily Telegraph*

V

GRANTA

HEINRICH BÖLL
GERMAN EFFICIENCY

German Efficiency

I hate the man who stood back to back with me for the hour-long journey from Düsseldorf to Cologne. I didn't see his face or his hands; I just felt his shoulder-blades and sometimes his elbows, when he explained something particularly keenly to his companion. He talked for the whole hour. His voice was quite impersonal—I would hardly recognize it again—and yet I hate him. I don't wish him dead, but I would like to see him spend the next two hundred years listening only to his own voice, a gramophone recording of his own words, the ones he spoke from Düsseldorf to Cologne. First it was currency reform, and from there it was German efficiency, which has been suppressed because there was no currency reform. But it couldn't be suppressed. No, nothing could suppress German efficiency and German workmanship. And German science and German soldiers. And the German armed forces and German confidence. And German toilet-seats. Nothing in the world could suppress all of that.

His companion didn't say much. He said 'yes'. He said 'that's right'; occasionally he said 'certainly'. A few times he said 'absolutely'. Once or twice 'quite, quite'. I don't want to leave anything out. German strength, too, and German forests and German art, the lot. The man's voice wasn't animated. It was as dry as the dust that coats the ruins of our houses. And as tasteless as our jam. It was as monotonous as the rattling of the train, which was crammed as full as a freight-car with room not only for eight horses but for forty people with luggage, people allowed to die. People who are permitted to die after they have been yelled at and humiliated enough.

I didn't have the courage to drink the sea dry and argue with this man: I was too tired and too despairing, and in the muggy darkness I couldn't even smoke a cigarette because there was a

Heinrich Böll wrote 'German Efficiency' in 1949. It was discovered in the Böll archives in Cologne last year, and published by Der Spiegel *in August 1992.*

Opposite: German refugees in Berlin, 1945.

Heinrich Böll

Above: Planning the new Dresden, 1946. The Allied raid on the city left 100,000 dead.

woman standing patiently in front of me with a rucksack full of potatoes on her back and I didn't want to burn her only coat. Perhaps, I thought, she'll need to use it to barter with a farmer; perhaps she could get another two hundredweight of potatoes for it, and perhaps farmers won't accept coats with holes in them. I couldn't burn two hundredweight of potatoes! No one could do that, not even a despairing man with German efficiency sinking deeper and deeper, like a terrible slow poison, into his guts, spreading into his veins and arteries and slowly paralyzing him so that he couldn't even begin to think of drinking the sea dry. German toilet-seats hung around his neck, not like life-belts, but like lead weights that would drag him down to the bottom of the luke-warm sea that he didn't have the courage to drink. And German workmanship simply nauseated him, and the German armed forces weighed on him, for many miles from Düsseldorf to Cologne, and German science sat disagreeably in his trousers like an attack of diarrhoea, which his sphincter, worn out and exhausted, was unable to regulate. Everything was relentlessly pulling him downwards.

But after Düsseldorf, that tepid city, when I finally had room to roll and even smoke a cigarette, I was afraid that the sea would one day come up to me because I hadn't tried to drink it dry, down to the last drop, the sea of stupidity, the whole sea of infinite German talkativeness, unmatched anywhere in the world.

Translated from the German by Shaun Whiteside

box office 071 730 1745
cc 071 836 2428

main house

until 6 march
king lear

by William Shakespeare directed by Max Stafford-Clark
The first Shakespeare production at the Royal Court since
Richard Eyre's Hamlet, *with Jonathan Pryce, in 1980.*

23 march – 3 april
fires in the mirror
written and performed by Anna Deavere Smith

from 15 april
playwright in new york
by Martin Crimp

theatre upstairs

9 january – 6 february
marching for fausa
by Biyi Bandele directed by Annie Castledine
Lying ministers, sexual scandal, and a government on the verge
of collapse in this first full-length play by Biyi Bandele

9 – 13 february
Gloria and the Royal Court Theatre present
night after night
written and performed by Neil Bartlett live music by Nicolas Bloomfield

16 – 27 february
The Royal Court Theatre presents Snarling Beasties' production of
out of the ordinary
by Debbie Isitt
A co-production with the Arts Centre, University of Warwick

other productions *- further information.081 960 4641*

week beginning 14 march
Commonwealth Institute
A promenade production, written by Deepak Verma, performed by
members of the Royal Court Young People's Theatre and the local
community exploring mythology from around the Commonwealth.

GRANTA

HANS MAGNUS ENZENSBERGER
THE GREAT MIGRATION

Two passengers in a railway compartment. They have commandeered the little tables, clothes-hooks and baggage-racks: made themselves at home. Newspapers, coats and handbags lie around on the empty seats. The door opens, and two new travellers enter. Their arrival is not welcomed. The original passengers, even if they do not know one another at all, behave with a remarkable degree of solidarity. There is a distinct reluctance to clear the free seats and let the newcomers share them. The compartment has become their territory to make available, and they regard each new person who comes in as an intruder. This behaviour cannot be rationally justified; it is more deeply rooted.

However, matters virtually never get to the point of open conflict. That is because the passengers are subject to a system of rules; their territorial instinct is curbed by the institutional code of the railroad as well as by other unwritten norms of behaviour: like that of courtesy. Looks are exchanged, and formulaic apologies are muttered through clenched teeth, but the new passengers are tolerated. One gets used to them. Yet they remain, even if to a decreasing degree, stigmatized.

This harmless model is not without its absurd features. The railway compartment is itself a transitory domicile, a location which serves only to change locations. The passenger is the negation of the sedentary person. He has traded a real territory for a virtual one. Despite this he defends his transient abode with sullen resentment.

Every migration, irrespective of its cause, nature and scale, leads to conflicts. Self-interest and xenophobia are anthropological constants: they are older than all known societies.

To avoid blood-baths and to make possible even a minimum of exchange between different clans, tribes and ethnic groups, ancient societies invented the rituals of hospitality. These provisions, however, do not abrogate the status of the stranger. Quite the reverse: they fix it. The guest is sacred, but he must not stay.

Photo: Jean Mohr

Two new passengers open the compartment door. From this instant, the status of those who entered earlier changes. Only a moment ago, they were the intruders; now they are natives. They belong to the clan of compartment-occupants and claim all the privileges due to them. The defence of such an 'ancestral' territory, that was only recently occupied, appears paradoxical; noteworthy is the absence of any empathy with the newcomers, who have to struggle against the same opposition, face the same difficult initiation, to which their predecessors were subjected. Curious, the rapidity with which one's own origin is concealed and denied.

Clan and tribal groups have existed since the earth was inhabited by human beings; nations have existed for only 200 years or so. It is not difficult to see the difference. Ethnic groups come into being semi-spontaneously, 'of their own accord'; nations are consciously created, and are often quite artificial entities, which cannot cohere without a specific ideology. This ideological foundation, together with its rituals and emblems (flags, anthems), originated in the nineteenth century. From Europe and North America, it has spread over the whole world.

A country that wants to succeed as a nation needs a well-coded self-consciousness, its own system of institutions (army, customs and excise, diplomatic corps) and numerous legal means of demarcating its boundaries (sovereignty, citizenship, passports). It is rarely managed without historical legends. If necessary, proof of a glorious past is forged, venerable traditions dreamed up. Usually the more artificial a nation's genesis, the more precarious and hysterical its national feeling. That holds true for the 'overdue nations' of Europe—the new states which emerged from the colonial system—as well as for forced unions like the former USSR and Yugoslavia, which have a tendency towards disintegration and civil war.

Of course, no nation has an absolutely homogenous ethnic population. This fact is in fundamental conflict with the national feeling which has taken shape in most states. Consequently, as a rule, the leading national group finds it difficult to reconcile itself to the existence of minorities, and every wave of immigrants appears to be a political problem. The most important exceptions to this pattern are those modern states which owe their existence to migration on a large scale; above all the United States, Canada and Australia. Their founding myth is the *tabula rasa*. (Though that depends on the extermination of the indigenous population.)

For almost all nations the distinction between 'our own' people and 'strangers' appears quite natural, even if utterly questionable historically. Whoever wishes to hold on to the distinction needs to maintain, by his own logic, that he has always been there—a thesis which can all too easily be disproved. A national history assumes the ability to forget everything not in accord with it.

External and self-ascription can never be made to coincide. The meaning of the sentence 'The Finns are cunning and drunken' depends on whether a Finn or a Swede is speaking. Consider the different reactions it provokes: among Finns only a Finn would be allowed to say it; coming from a Swede it would cause a scandal. Such differences always conceal a long history of contact and conflict.

Contemporary migrations differ from earlier movements of people in more than one respect. First, mobility has increased enormously in the past two centuries. The developing world market has required global mobilization and imposed it by force where necessary, as with the opening of Japan and China in the nineteenth century. Capital tears down national barriers. It

Overleaf: War veterans and young 'comrades' in Wursiedel, Bavaria, listen to a speech by neo-Nazi leader, Michael Kuhnen.

Photo: Sacha Hartgers (Focus/Matrix)

disregards patriotic and racist impulses, but can make tactical use of them if necessary. In general, though, the tendency is for the free movement of capital to draw labour behind it, without regard to race or nationality. With the globalization of the world market (which was completed only very recently), the new migratory movements will probably take the place of state-organized colonial wars and expeditions of conquest. Whereas electronic money follows only its own logic and playfully overcomes every resistance, human beings act as if they were subject to some incomprehensible compulsion. Their embarkations are like movements of flight, which it would be cynical to call voluntary.

No one emigrates without the promise of something better. In early times legend and rumour were the media of hope. The Promised Land, legendary Atlantis, El Dorado, the New World provided the magical stories that motivated many to set out. Today it is the high-frequency images which the global media system transmits to the very last village of the developing world. These images have less substance, less reality, than even the most marvellous ancient legends; however, their effects are incomparably more powerful. Advertising, which is effortlessly understood in its wealthy countries of origin as an empty sign without a real referent, counts in the Second and Third Worlds as a reliable description of a possible way of life. To a large extent it determines the horizon of expectations prompting migration.

For centuries the world's population fluctuated regularly, but never increased significantly. However, since the world's population has begun to grow exponentially, the rules of the game have changed. Sooner or later the unimaginable quantitative increase must have an effect on the quality of the migratory movements.

That this is already the case is doubtful. Today it is estimated that more than twenty million immigrants live in Western Europe. The flow of refugees in Africa and Asia is on a similar scale. These are large numbers. But if one considers that between 1810 and 1921 thirty-four million people, mainly from Europe, emigrated to the United States alone, then it is hardly possible to argue that these figures are unprecedented. Indeed, it could even be claimed that modern migration has, so far, been rather limited, especially if measured against the absolute increase in the world's population (the United Nations forecasts estimates a growth of almost one billion for 1990–2000). This invites the conclusion that only a small fraction of the potential migrants has actually set itself in motion: the real migration of peoples is still to come.

The media approach this conclusion fatalistically and illustrate it with fantastic doom. A strange enjoyment of fear emerges from the apocalyptic pictures they project. All the present-day phenomena of crisis—the unstable condition of the world economy, the huge technological dangers, the disintegration of the Soviet empire, the ecological threat —provoke scenarios of this kind. Possibly the anticipatory panic even serves as immunization, a kind of psychic inoculation. At any rate it leads not to solutions but, at best, policies of stop- and-go, alternating between timid repair measures and obstacles to thought and action.

A life-boat is packed with shipwreck survivors. In the stormy sea around it there are other people in danger of going under. How should the occupants of the boat behave? Should they push away or hack off the hands of the next person who grabs the side of the boat? Or pull him on and let the boat sink? The dilemma is part of the standard repertoire of casuistry. The moral philosophers who discuss it usually pay no attention to the fact that they themselves are safely on dry land. Yet all abstract reflections founder on just this 'as if', no matter what their conclusion. The best intention is frustrated by the cosiness of the seminar room, because no one can credibly declare how he would behave in an emergency.

The parable of the life-boat is reminiscent of the railway compartment model. It is that model taken to its extreme. Here, also, travellers act as if they were property owners, with the difference that the ancestral territory they defend is a drifting nutshell and that it is no longer a matter of comfort but of life and death.

It is of course no accident that the image of the life-boat recurs in the political discourse about immigration, usually in the form of the assertion, 'The boat is full.' That this sentence is factually inaccurate is the least that can be said about it. A look around is enough to disprove it, as those who use it know. But they are not interested in its truthfulness; they like the fears it conjures up. Evidently many West Europeans believe that their lives are endangered. They compare their situation to that of shipwreck survivors. Suddenly those who have a roof over their heads imagine that they are *boat people*, emigrants sailing steerage, Albanians on an overcrowded ghost ship. The distress at sea which is hallucinated in this way is presumably intended to justify behaviour which is only conceivable in extreme situations. From here it is not a very big step to hacking off hands.

There is something comforting about the railway compartment analogy, simply because the location of the action is so restricted. Even in the terrifying image of the life-boat individual human beings can still be recognized—as in Géricault's painting 'The Raft of the Medusa', where eighteen individual faces, and their fates, can be distinguished. Contemporary statistics, whether they are referring to the starving, the unemployed or refugees, express everything in millions. These are numbers which paralyse the imagination. The aid organizations and their campaign managers know that these numbers are incomprehensible, which is why they always show only a single child with huge pathetic eyes, so as to make the catastrophe commensurable to our compassion. But the terror of the big number is without eyes. Empathy breaks

Photo: Ali Paczensky (Zenit/Select)

Opposite: Russian Jewish children in a refugee hostel, Berlin.

down before such excessive demand, and reason is made aware of its impotence.

> Superfluous, superfluous . . . an excellent word I've come up with. The deeper I plunge into myself and the closer I examine the whole of my past life, the more I am convinced of the harsh truth of that expression. Superfluous—precisely so. The word does not apply to other people . . . People are good and evil, intelligent and stupid, pleasant and unpleasant; but superfluous?

It would not have occurred to Ivan Turgenev's hero Chulkaturin to regard his wet-nurse, the coachman, the peasants on the estate—still less whole villages, regions, peoples and continents—as superfluous; he talks rather of his father, a landowner, with his country houses, and of himself, with his boredom, his loneliness and his disgust—'The word does not apply to other people,' he thinks.

One hundred and fifty years after his demise Chulkaturin's situation seems altogether idyllic. Of course there have been great massacres and endemic poverty in every age. Enemies were enemies, and the poor were poor; yet only since history has become world history have whole peoples seen themselves condemned to superfluousness. The judges who pass this sentence go under the names of 'colonialism', 'industrialization', 'final solution', 'Versailles' or 'Yalta', and their decrees are pronounced openly and put into practice systematically, so that no one can be in any doubt what fate is intended for him: emigration, expulsion or genocide.

Though state-organized crime is still widespread, more virulent is the overarching anonymous instance of 'the world market'. It declares ever larger sections of mankind to be superfluous, not through political persecution, by command of the Führer or party resolution, but spontaneously, as it were, by its own logic. The result is no less murderous, but the guilty can never be brought to book. In the language of economics that means: an enormously increasing supply of human beings is faced by a clearly declining demand. Even in wealthy societies people are daily rendered superfluous. What should be done with them?

The logical status of hallucinations allows that two mutually exclusive realities can find room in the same brain. So it is that many supporters of the life-boat model are simultaneously obsessed by a delusion which expresses precisely the opposite fear: 'The Germans (French, Swedes, Italians) are dying out.' Long-term extrapolations of current population statistics are produced to serve as the shaky basis of these slogans. Even though such forecasts have repeatedly proved false in the past, terrible consequences are predicted: an ageing population, decadence, depopulation—accompanied by concerned glances at economic growth, tax revenue and the pension system.

The idea that too many and too few people could simultaneously exist in the same territory causes panic—an affliction for which I would like to suggest the term *demographic bulimia*.

Analyses from those far-off times when an attempt was made to advance a political economy of migration appear quite comforting in their sobriety compared to the delirious ramblings of the present day. At the turn of the century the American economist Richmond Mayo Smith offered a model example of such cool-headed reflection:

> The amount of money brought by the immigrants is not large, and is probably more than offset by the money sent back by immigrants for the support of families and friends at home or to aid them in following. The valuable element is the able-bodied immigrant himself as a factor of production. It is said, for instance, that an adult slave used to be valued at from $800 to $1,000, so that every adult immigrant may be looked upon as worth that sum to the country. Or it has been said that an adult immigrant represents what it would cost to bring up a child from infancy, to the age, say, of fifteen. This has been estimated by Ernst Engel as amounting to $550 for a German child. The most scientific procedure,

however, is to calculate the probable earnings of the immigrant during the rest of his 'lifetime', and deduct these from his expenses of living. The remainder represents his net earnings which he will contribute to the well-being of the new country. W. Farr reckoned this to be, in the case of unskilled English emigrants, about £175. Multiplying the total number of adult immigrants, we get the annual value of immigration. Such attempts to put a precise money value on immigration are futile. They neglect the question of quality and of opportunity. The immigrant is worth what it has cost to bring him up only if he is able-bodied, honest and willing to work. If he is diseased, crippled, dishonest or indolent, he may be a direct loss to the community instead of a gain. So, too, the immigrant is worth his future net earnings to the community only if there is a demand for his labor.

For a long time there was greater anxiety in Europe about the consequences of emigration than of immigration. This debate stretches back into the eighteenth century. The concept of population as wealth derives from mercantilism. In those days emigration was regarded as a haemorrhage, and the attempt was made to limit, even forbid it. In many states, emigrating, or making it possible for others to emigrate, was subject to severe punishment, a practice which communist states adhered to until very recently. Louis XIV had borders carefully watched in order to keep his subjects in, and in England there was a ban on the emigration of qualified artisans until the middle of the nineteenth century. The so-called Free or Departure Money, an emigration tax imposed on the estates of emigrants, was in force in Germany until 1817, and the Nazis utilized this confiscatory procedure when they did not yet want to murder the Jews, but only expel them.

Ireland is the classic example of a country of emigration. Brutal exploitation by the English led, in the 1840s, to a catastrophic famine, from which the country has not recovered even today. In 1843 Ireland had a population of eight and a half million; in 1961 this figure had sunk to less than three million. In the period from 1851 to 1901 an average of seventy-two per cent of all Irish people emigrated. Ireland remains one of the poorest countries in Western Europe. One can beat one's brains for a long time over the question of whether emigration is to blame for its poverty, or whether, on the contrary, it improved the situation of the inhabitants.

A naïve but illuminating conclusion is drawn by the anonymous contributor to a lexicon dating from 1843:

> Emigration is weak as a remedy against pauperism. If today one could remove all the poor from the lands visited by pauperism, then there would be, should its causes continue to be active, just as many again in twenty years, perhaps in ten. In the main the state should strive to establish and maintain such conditions within its borders, so that at least destitution and dissatisfaction do not drive the people forth.

Emigrants never represent a cross-section of the whole population. 'It is the man of energy, of some means, of ambition, who takes the chances of success in the new country, leaving the poor, the indolent, the weak and crippled at home.' wrote Mayo Smith. 'It is maintained that such emigration institutes a process of selection which is not favorable to the home country.'

This thesis is persuasive. The brain drain, a kind of demographic flight of capital, has devastating effects on countries like China and India, but also on the former Soviet Union. It was of considerable importance in the collapse of East Germany.

A large proportion of the Iranian intelligentsia has emigrated in recent decades. The number of doctors from the Third World working in Western Europe exceeds the number of aid workers who are sent to Asia, Africa and Latin America—where there is a shortage of trained doctors—from the states of the European Community.

Better qualified immigrants encounter fewer barriers. The Indian astro-physicist, the star Chinese architect, the Black African Nobel Prize-winner are welcome all over the world. The rich are never mentioned in this context anyway; no one questions their freedom of movement. For businessmen from Hong Kong the acquisition of a British passport is no problem. Swiss citizenship, too, is, for immigrants from any country whatsoever, only a question of price. No one has ever objected to the colour of the Sultan of Brunei's skin. Drug and arms dealers recognize no distinctions of race and are far above nationalism. Where the bank accounts look good, xenophobia disappears as if by magic. But strangers are all the stranger if they are poor.

Of course, the poor are not a homogeneous society either. In all rich countries there are complicated procedures for the control of immigration. They favour those among the poor with very particular characteristics—valued in capitalism—such as knowledge of the world, determination, flexibility and criminal verve. These virtues are indispensable for overcoming bureaucratic obstacles. In other situations sheer physical strength counts. It was only the youngest and strongest of the Albanians who could hold their own against the Italian authorities.

Mayo Smith again: 'On the other side, it is said that the men who are doing well at home are the ones least likely to emigrate, because they have the least to gain. It is therefore the restless, the unsuccessful, or at least those not fitted for the strenuous competition of the older countries, who are tempted to go.'

Opposite: Turkish workers awaiting the results of medicals to allow them to work in Germany.

Photo: Jean Mohr

31

That there is some truth in this is demonstrated by the credulous victims of the organized gangs who smuggle people from Asia, Africa and Eastern Europe. They usually have not the least idea of what awaits them. Once arrived, these travellers seem apathetic, as if they had long ago abandoned every hope.

Black markets flourish everywhere there are restrictions. They equalize pressure between supply and demand, without regard for laws, regulations and ethical norms. Since in the real world there are no completely closed systems, illegal transactions can be impeded by controls but never quite prevented. So an illegal trade in human beings has developed in all wealthy countries. However, whereas in classic black markets higher prices are always obtained than in legal trade, the black market in labour follows the reverse logic. Lack does not rule here, but superfluity. Superfluous people are cheap. Clandestine immigration reduces the price of labour.

However, each illegally employed immigrant presupposes an illegally operating entrepreneur. The shadow economy usually works closely with criminal groups that smuggle human beings. In the textile industry, the unskilled sector and, above all, the building trade, practices dominate which are reminiscent of the slave markets of the past.

In some parts of the United States and in the Mediterranean countries of Europe, the shadow economy has so much political power that it is in a position to exert considerable pressure on government. In Germany the authorities turn two blind eyes to illegal employment. Regulations which are supposed to stem immigration are surreptitiously sabotaged, and curious forms of compromise arise.

The size of these slave markets is unknown. No one has any interest in discovering it. The only certain thing is that the unknown figures are very high. In the United States, estimates suggest there are several million illegal immigrants, mostly from

Opposite: Hostel for asylum-seekers, Brandenburg.

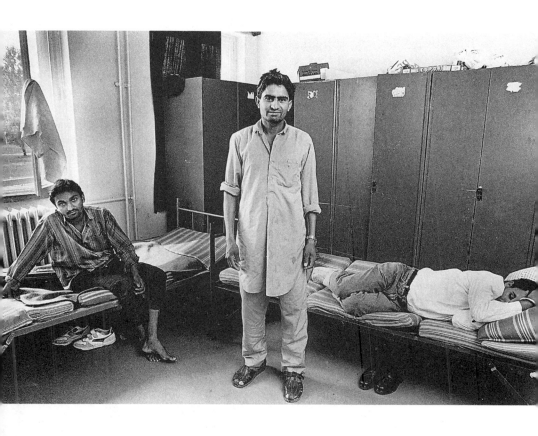

Mexico; in Italy, more than a million. Wherever one looks closely it becomes evident that the officially proclaimed 'policy towards foreigners' rests on a series of deliberate self-deceptions.

A question arises: does the Great Migration represent a solution, and if so, to which problem? To mention a crude example, would Albania be helped if the active half of its population was admitted to other countries? 'It is evident [from these arguments] that no general answer can be given to this question.' That is the amply general conclusion to which Richmond Mayo Smith came in his day. A hundred years later there is little else to add.

Asylum is an ancient convention of sacred origin. It owes its name to the Greeks, though the convention can also be demonstrated in many other tribal societies. It persisted during the Middle Ages: criminals and debtors who had taken refuge in a church could be delivered up to secular justice only with the consent of the bishop. In more recent times, this custom has been increasingly restricted in the Protestant countries. With the modern legal code it has disappeared altogether.

In international law, the first places of asylum were embassies, a tradition maintained until today, notably in Latin America. From the expanded concept of sovereignty, the nation states derived the right to take in non-citizens, who were being politically persecuted in their homeland, and refuse to surrender them. In this case, asylum is not the right of the refugee but of the receiving state. Representative cases of this practice include the rebellious Poles, as well as revolutionaries like Garibaldi, Kossuth, Louis Blanc, Bakunin and Mazzini, who were regarded as criminals in their countries of origin but not infrequently celebrated as heroes in the countries that took them in.

The refugees, whom in Germany we call asylum-seekers or *Asylanten*—asylants—usually have little in common with such historical figures. Contemporary linguistic usage is influenced by quite another meaning which the word assumed in the Victorian period:

The most frequently occurring asylums, the need for which makes itself felt chiefly in the big cities, are the following: i) for drunkards (inebriates' homes); ii) for prostitutes (often called Magdalene Foundations); iii) for released prisoners, who are lacking employment; iv) for poor women in childbed; v) asylums for the homeless.

Such places of custody have nothing to do with the original meaning of asylum. They are intended not for strangers to the land, but for stigmatized locals. The only thing these people share with our *Asylanten* is their poverty.

The idea of asylum has always been ambiguous. Concerns of expediency and ethics, often influenced by religion, have become so muddled that they are difficult to disentangle. In the beginning asylum pertained to robbery, murder and killing: within a clan there was no other sanction but revenge, and whoever did not belong had no rights; asylum—etymologically, the place where one was not robbed—was a makeshift, created in order to meet a need and to make communication beyond tribal boundaries possible.

The immunity of asylum, that is, holds for both guilty and innocent, criminals and victims alike. The moral ambiguity is evident even in the present day. One only needs to think of figures like Pol Pot in Peking, Idi Amin in Libya, Marcos in Hawaii or Stroessner in Brazil, to say nothing of the numerous Nazis, who with the help of the Vatican found refuge in Latin America. Originally this practice may have represented an attempt to provide overthrown rulers with the option of retreat, lessening the risk of civil war. However, as the Cambodian example shows, the granting of asylum can also serve the aim of keeping conflicts alive.

Overleaf: Vietnamese hostel, Malchow, east Germany.

Photo: Gust (Zenit/Select)

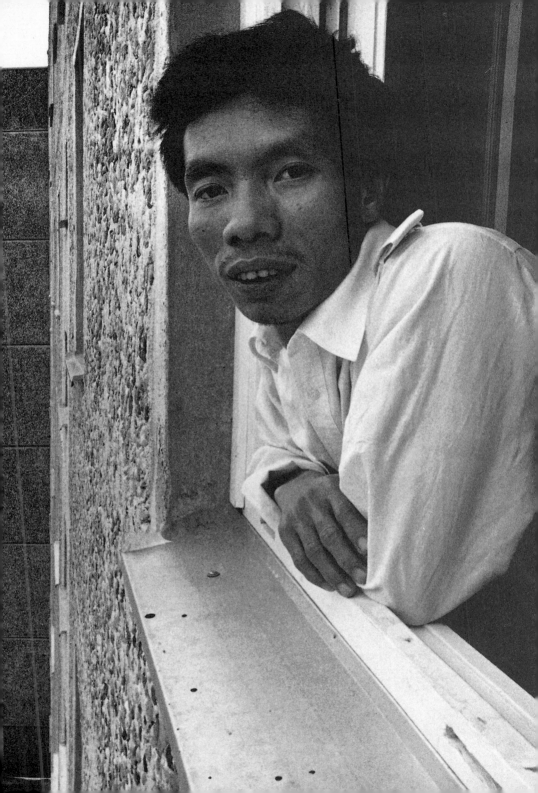

The 'noble' asylum seeker is a nineteenth-century idea. In history he is the exception.

Confusing the right to asylum with other questions of immigration and emigration has fatal consequences. The social and political expansion of the concept of asylum has made the muddle greater. It is not clear why immigrants should be equated with overthrown dictators and criminals on the run or with alcoholics and tramps. In this way the 'asylum-seeker' has become a discriminatory, negatively loaded term, a political football.

This confusion, however, turns against those who contrived it, because it contradicts the fundamental idea of asylum to separate the good from the bad, to decide who is a 'genuine' asylum-seeker and who is not. The distinction between economic refugees and the politically persecuted is often impossible to draw, and a law which attempts to do so will inevitably be embarrassed. After all, the war between winners and losers is carried out not only with bombs and automatic rifles. Corruption, indebtedness, flight of capital, hyper-inflation, exploitation, ecological catastrophes, religious fanaticism and sheer incompetence can provide as solid ground for flight as the the direct threat of prison, torture or shooting.

Germany is a country that owes its present population to huge movements of migration. Since earliest times there has been a constant exchange of population groups for the most diverse reasons. Because of their geographical position, the Germans, just like the Austrians, are an especially varied people. That blood- and race-ideologies gained credibility here, of all places, can be understood as a kind of compensation to prop up an especially fragile national identity. The Aryan was never anything more than a risible construct. (To that extent German racism is different from Japanese racism which appeals to the relatively high degree of ethnic homogeneity of the island population.)

The Second World War mobilized the Germans in more than one sense. Not only did the majority of the male population swarm out as far as the North Cape and the Caucasus (and, as prisoners of war, as far as Siberia and New England), not to mention nearly the whole Jewish population who were forced into emigration and death, but Germany also abducted more than ten million labourers, a third of them women, from all over Europe, so that thirty per cent of all jobs, and in the armaments industry more than half, were done by foreigners. After the war, there were millions of displaced persons; only very few remained in Germany. Compared to these catastrophic movements all contemporary turbulences appear harmless.

Further large-scale migrations began at the end of the war. The number of refugees who, between 1945 and 1950, came into the four occupied zones is estimated at twelve million; in addition there were more than three million 'resettlements' from Eastern Europe and the Soviet Union of people who are considered to be of German origin. Between 1944 and 1989, 4.4 million went to the West from the former East Germany. And then, from the mid-1950s, the systematic recruitment of labour migrants—the *Gästarbeiter*—began which is the principal reason for more than five million foreigners having their legal place of residence in Germany. (The proportion of foreigners is still well below the level recorded by the German Empire before the First World War.) Until the 1980s, the right to asylum was an infinitesimally minor factor in these population movements.

It is puzzling that a population that has had such experiences in its own lifetime can suffer from the delusion that the current migration is a new phenomenon. It is as if Germans had fallen victim to the amnesia observed in the railway passenger model. They are in effect the new arrivals who, having secured their own seat, then insist on enjoying the rights of those who have been there for ever. As is well known, the consequences are more significant than those of a first-class compartment made slightly crowded. Since 1991 there has been an organized manhunt.

Xenophobia—a specifically German problem? That would be too good to be true. The solution would be obvious: isolate the Federal Republic, and the rest of the world could heave a sigh of relief. It would be easy to refer to some neighbouring countries where immigration qualifications are considerably more rigorous than in Germany. But such comparisons are sterile. Xenophobia is a universal phenomenon, and nowhere is it approached rationally. What then is so special about the Germans?

The historical guilt feelings of the Germans, no matter how well founded, are not a sufficient explanation. The causes go further back. They lie in the precarious self-consciousness of the nation. It is a fact that Germans cannot tolerate each other—or even themselves: witness the emotions aroused by German unification. Do these people strike you as the kind who are ready to love their neighbours?

This condition of self-loathing is evident not only in the hostility to foreigners, but also in the opposition to it. Nowhere is a universalist rhetoric more highly valued than in Germany. The immigrant is defended in a tone of utter moralizing self-righteousness: 'Foreigners, don't leave us alone with the Germans!' or 'Never again Germany!'. Immigrants are idealized in a manner reminiscent of philo-Semitism. Self-hatred is projected on to others—most notably in the insidious assertion 'I am a foreigner,' which numerous German 'celebrities' have adopted.

It is a curious alliance between the remnants of the Left and the clergy (a similar alliance can also be observed in Scandinavia, which suggests that the stance has something to do with the political culture of Protestantism). While preaching the Sermon on the Mount is the duty of the church, it can't be passed off as a political solution: whoever calls upon his fellow citizens to offer shelter to all the weary and wretched of the earth—often with reference to collective crimes which stretch from the conquest of America to the Holocaust—without consideration of the economic consequences or regard for whether such a project is realizable, loses all political credibility. He becomes incapable of action. Deep-seated social conflicts cannot be healed by sermons.

How many immigrants can a country accommodate? There are too many variables to answer this question but economics provide the best guide-lines. The unavoidable conflicts that arise from large-scale migration are intensified when there is chronic unemployment in the countries of destination. In times of full employment, which will probably never return, millions of labour migrants were recruited. Ten million immigrants came to the United States from Mexico; three million to France from the Maghreb; five million to the Federal Republic, among them almost two million Turks. The migration was not only tolerated, it was emphatically welcomed. The attitude changed only as unemployment increased, even though this was at a time of growing prosperity. Since then the immigrants' opportunities on the labour market have dwindled. Many are facing a career on the dole. In the face of virtually insurmountable bureaucratic barriers, others have to live illegally; the only prospects open to them are the shadow economy and criminality: prejudice becomes a self-fulfiling prophecy.

A further, underestimated obstacle to immigration is the welfare state. In contrast to America, where no newcomer can count on a social net to catch him, the inhabitants of many European states can claim the minimal safeguards of unemployment benefit, health care and social security.

But the welfare state is under ever-increasing pressure, the safety net has come to be perceived as an association of paying members: its long-term financing is uncertain.

Today there is no point in trying to show that the newcomers are contributors to, as well as users of, the welfare state, or that immigration can have a beneficial effect on the age structure of the population: there is no point because the argument requires a labour market able to absorb the immigrants. In any case, many demographers believe that immigration would have to reach enormous proportions in order to restore the traditional age pyramid. Depending on the model used, it has been estimated that for this goal to be achieved four to ten million younger immigrants per annum would be required for the United States and at least one million for the Germany—and Germany could not cope with such an influx, either politically or economically.

Things may get worse. What group is now ready or capable of being integrated with others? The multicultural society remains a confusing slogan as long as the difficulties which it throws up, and fails to clarify, remain taboo. If no one knows, or wants to know, what culture means—'Everything that humans do and do not do' seems to be the most precise definition available—the debate will lead nowhere.

The experiences provided by large-scale migrations in the past are ignored in such discussions. The opponents of immigration deny the examples of success which could be found everywhere, from the Swedes in Finland to the Huguenots, from the Poles in the Ruhr to the Hungarian refugees of 1956. The advocates will not hear of the failures: the civil wars in the Lebanon, in Yugoslavia and in the Caucasus or the conflicts in the American cities. The idea of a multinational state has seldom proved durable. It is perhaps asking too much that anyone remember the disintegration of the Ottoman Empire or the Habsburg Monarchy. But as far as the Soviet Union is concerned, no knowledge whatsoever of history is required; a television is enough. For decades the idea of a Soviet 'multicultural society' was inculcated, with a sense of belonging and common goals. The result was an implosion with incalculable consequences.

Dangers can also be observed in the classic countries of immigration. For a long time the new arrivals showed themselves extremely willing to adapt, even if it is doubtful whether the famous 'melting pot' ever existed. Most immigrants were well able to distinguish between integration and assimilation. They accepted the written and unwritten norms of the society which

Opposite: Bus carrying immigrant workers, Hoyerswerda.

Photos: Detlev Konnerth (Fotoagentur Lichtblick)

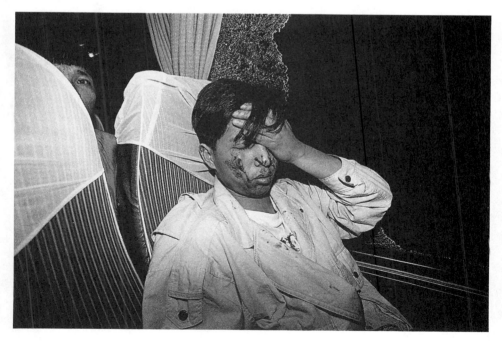

took them in, but held on to their cultural tradition—and often also to their language and religious customs—for a long time.

Today it is impossible to count on such an attitude among the old minorities or the new immigrants. Poverty and discrimination, especially in the United States, but also in Great Britain and France, have led more and more groups in the population to insist on their 'identity'. It is by no means clear what such an insistence is supposed to mean. Militant spokesmen raise separatist demands. At times the slogans fall back on the legacy of tribalism: a Black 'nation', an Islamic 'nation'; in England there is a 'Muslim Parliament'. Many Blacks in the United States believe that the drug trade is a calculated strategy of the Whites with the aim of exterminating the Black minority.

There are confrontations not only with the majority, but also between the minorities. African-Americans fight against Jews, Latinos against Koreans, Haitians against local Blacks. In some city districts there are virtual tribal wars, and in extreme cases local demagogues claim apartheid as a human right and the conversion of the ghetto into a separate state as their ultimate goal.

Even if the immigrants' readiness to integrate is decreasing, they are not the ones provoking; conflict originates in the natives. If only 'natives' meant simply skinheads and neo-Nazis! But the gangs form only the violent, self-appointed vanguard of xenophobia. The goal of integration has not yet been accepted by large parts of the European population. The majority is not ready for it, indeed at present not even capable of it.

A recent argument against immigration derives, interestingly, from the arsenal of anti-colonialism. Algeria for the Algerians, Cuba for the Cubans, Tibet for the Tibetans, Africa for the Africans—such slogans which helped many liberation movements to victory are now also taken up by Europeans, and not without a certain insidious logic.

It is possible to see, in the idea of a 'preventive migration policy', which is intended to remove the causes of emigration, a philanthropic variant of this idea. For that to be successful, it would be necessary to remove the gap between poor and rich countries or at least to reduce it considerably. The task is beyond the economic capacity of the industrial nations, even leaving aside questions of political will and the ecological limits to growth.

That anyone can say out loud what he thinks of the government or the state or the Lord above without being tortured and threatened with death; that disagreements are settled before a court and not by a blood feud; that women can move freely and are not forced to sell themselves or be circumcised; that one can cross the street without being caught in the machine-gun fire of a rampaging soldiery: these things are indispensable. Everywhere in the world the majority want such conditions, and are ready to defend them where they prevail. Without being over-emphatic, one can say these are the minimum conditions of civilization.

In the history of humanity this minimum has been achieved only exceptionally and temporarily. Whoever wants to defend it from external challenges faces a dilemma: the more fiercely civilization defends itself against an external threat and raises walls around itself, the less, in the end, it has left to defend. However, as far as the barbarians are concerned, we need not expect them at the gates. They are always already with us.

The Manhunt

Anyone who intervenes in the political discourses of German public life does so at his own risk. The moral accusations are not the deterrent: they are a proper function of journalism. It is the intellectual risk. Participants in a media debate will nearly always be reduced intellectually, if not made to appear foolish, by the simple fact of their contribution. The reason is not hard to find: whoever submits to the premises of a chat-show is already lost,

Overleaf: *Nationalistichen Front* meeting, Wewelsburg.

and has only himself to blame! It is no secret where the rules, to which the participants more or less cheerfully subordinate themselves, come from.

Political debate, which has become more and more ephemeral, evaporates on television, especially where television is at its 'most serious': the daily news report on political developments in Bonn. Opposition founders in such conditions: it becomes content with turning the slogans of the opponent on their head.

Nowhere does this crude pattern emerge more clearly than in the 'policy towards foreigners' and in the 'asylum debate'. (Even these formulations are themselves evidence of the Bonn dung-heap.) Politicians have circumvented this argument in two ways: on the one hand, an abstract moralizing discussion of principles; on the other, complex questions of legal procedure (which are raised when abstractions are exhausted and the prospect of actually doing something is suggested).

Through this strategy, elementary, obvious questions, evidently not in the interests of the politicians to ask, fall by the wayside.

I would like to raise one such question here, which, even if it is not central to the problem of the Great Migration, is a matter of life and death for those who live in Germany—whatever their passport or stamp or legitimacy. It is the question of whether the country is actually habitable. (I call a place uninhabitable where a gang of thugs is allowed to attack a person in the middle of the street or set fire to his house.) Is it possible to live with people who set out on organized manhunts?

My question has nothing to do with the so-called foreigners' problem or with new regulations for the asylum procedure or with the misery of the Third World or with ubiquitous racism. At stake is the monopoly of force which the state claims for itself.

One can accuse the various governments in the history of this republic of all kinds of things, but no one can say that they ever hesitated to make use of this monopoly of might if it seemed threatened. On the contrary, the executive has never lacked eagerness. Federal Frontier Police, secret services, security task forces, police mobile rapid response units, state and federal detective units have always been on hand with computer dragnets

Photo: Gust (Zenit/Select)

and helicopter squadrons, identikit pictures and armoured personnel carriers. And the legislature has been no less reticent. It has been game to the point of irresponsibility, constantly breaking new legal ground, drafting a law of 'criminal association' or banning visits and letters to prisoners awaiting trial.

But in the past months not even the most insignificant use has been made of this arsenal of repression. Indeed, the police and the courts have responded to the mass-scale appearance of gangs of thugs with a previously unheard of restraint. Arrests have been the exception; when carried out, culprits have almost always been set free the following day. The Federal State Prosecutor's Office and the Federal CID, once omnipresent in the media, devoted to repelling any threats to the German people, have kept silent; it's as if they have been temporarily retired. The Federal Frontier Police, which only a few years ago occupied every second crossroads, seems to have disappeared.

The politicians, meanwhile, have taken the stage in a new role: they've become social workers. There have been pleas for understanding the harsh reality of unemployment; we have been asked to view the killers as being 'culturally disorientated' or as 'poor swine' who must be treated with the utmost patience. After all, it is hardly possible to expect such underprivileged persons to realize that setting fire to children is, strictly speaking, not permissible. Attention must be drawn all the more urgently to the inadequate supply of leisure activities available to the arsonists.

Such sympathy is astonishing, when one remembers the pictures from Brokdorf (the power station which became the focus of anti-nuclear protest) and Startbahn West (a new runway at Frankfurt Airport, primarily for US military use). At that time, those responsible did not appear to regard the rapid development of discothèques and youth clubs as providing the solution; evidently, in the seventies, uncontested free access to the paradise of leisure society had not yet become an inalienable human right. On the contrary, beating, kicking and shooting were performed with considerable vigour and, if I remember rightly, the state was quite prepared to take a couple of dead in its stride.

Is the sudden change of heart due to a conversion? Since the Enlightenment there have always been humanitarians assuring us that the criminal law is an unsuitable solution to social problems. That can hardly be denied, given the conditions in the jails and the high rate of recidivism, even if the reformers still owe us a convincing alternative. However, the puzzling shift of the state apparatus towards sympathetic lenience for killers is not to be explained in this way. Shoplifters and bank robbers, confidence tricksters and embezzlers, terrorists and extortionists are being sent down as they always have been; no political party has as yet advocated the abolition of the penal code or, even, a thorough reform of the penal system. How, then, do we explain the bewildering gap between enthusiastic prosecution of certain crimes and this new *laissez faire* approach to others?

Is it possible that the intensity of the effort depends on the interests which the law exists to protect? In the precedents already mentioned it was a matter of the private ownership of real estate, of the right to enlarge airports, build motorways and erect nuclear installations of every kind. In the attacks of recent months, however, the lives of a few thousand inhabitants of the country were at stake. Evidently the agencies of the state consider murder and manslaughter a mere breach of the law, while the removal of a fence is a serious crime.

The circumstances invite other interpretations: is it possible that there are politicians who sympathize with the murderous gangs roaming the country? Is it possible that many observe the manhunt impassively because they imagine that such an attitude could be politically advantageous? One does not, of course, like to believe in such a degree of idiocy, and only the absence of other plausible explanations justifies considering it.

Even the most stupid person, however, should grasp one thing: renouncing the state's monopoly of force has consequences which might harm the political class itself. One consequence is the necessity for self-protection. If the state refuses to protect threatened individuals or groups, the threatened individuals or groups will have to arm themselves. And, as soon as the resistance has adequately organized itself, there will be gang wars (a development that can already be observed in Berlin and Hamburg). We will all recognize the political conditions: they are the same that Germany experienced towards the end of the Weimar Republic.

Translated from the German by Martin Chalmers

Photos overleaf: Sacha Hartgers (Focus/Matrix)

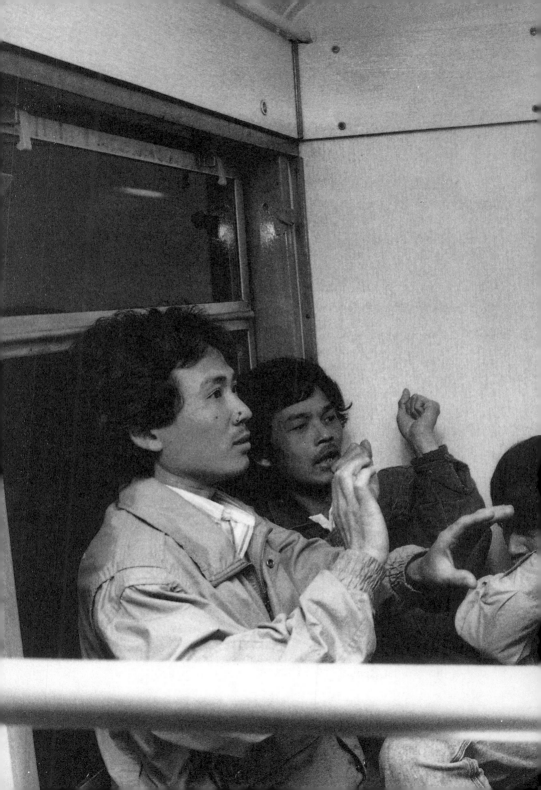

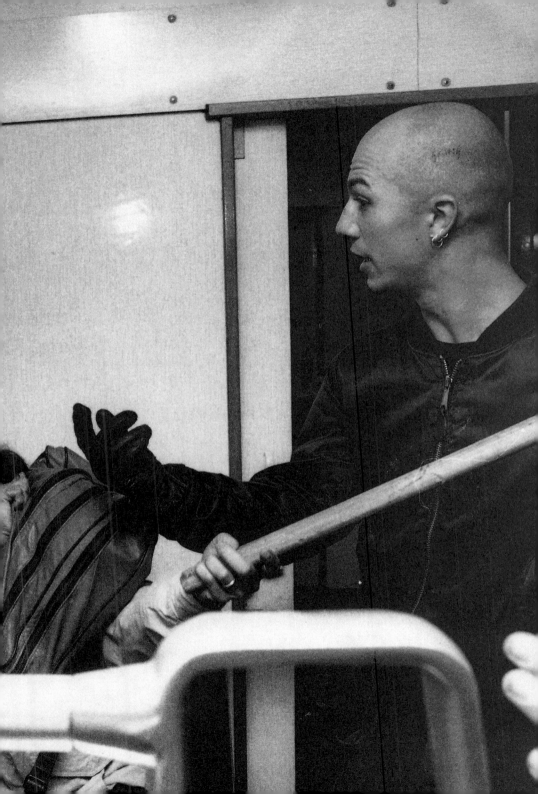

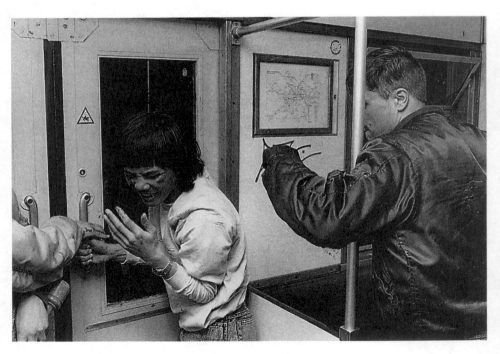

Subway, East Berlin.

GRANTA

CHRISTA WOLF
LIBERATION DAY

I've forgotten what my grandmother was wearing the time that nasty word 'Asia' got her back on her feet. The bomber squadrons, which now passed overhead in broad daylight on their way to Berlin, were already out of earshot. Someone had pushed open the door of the air-raid shelter, and in the bright triangle of sunlight at the entrance stood a pair of knee-high black military boots, and in them an SS officer, whose blond brain had registered every single word my grandmother had uttered during the long air-raid alarm: 'No, no, I'm not budging from here, I don't care if they kill me, one old woman more or less won't matter.'

'What?' said the SS officer. 'Tired of living? You'd rather fall into the hands of those Asian hordes? Don't you know that the Russians lop women's breasts off?'

That brought my grandmother wheezing to her feet. 'Oh, God,' she said, 'what has humanity done to deserve this?'

'Are you starting up again!' bellowed my grandfather. Now I can see them clearly, walking into the courtyard and taking up their positions alongside our handcart: Grandmother in her fine black coat; on her head the brown striped kerchief which my children still wear when they have a sore throat; Grandfather, wearing a cap with ear flaps and a herring-bone jacket. Time is short, the night is drawing near, closing in along with the enemy, although from a different direction: night from the west and the enemy from the east. In the south, flames rage against the sky. We imagine we can decipher the fiery script. The writing on the sky seems clear and spells out: Go west.

We tried to follow the country road but strayed from it in the darkness, groping about on side paths until we finally came upon a tree-lined drive leading towards a gate and a secluded estate. There was a crooked, slightly shaky man who was limping to the stables in the middle of the night—Kalle, he was called. He was not given to wondering at anything and so addressed the desperate, exhausted little troop in his particular, indifferent manner: Well, folks, Sodom and Gomorrah? Never mind. There's always room in the smallest cabin for a happy, loving couple.

Opposite: Walnienburg, 18 April 1945. German refugees were forbidden by the Allies from using the roads.

The man is not so bright, my mother said uneasily, as we followed Kalle across the courtyard, and my grandfather, who never said much, declared with satisfaction, He is pretty crazy in his head. And so he was. Kalle called my grandfather boss, he who had held no higher rank in his lifetime than that of private in the Kaiser's infantry regiment, cobbler's apprentice under Herr Lebüse in Bromberg, and signalman for the German Reich in the administrative district of Frankfurt (Oder). Boss, said Kalle, it's best if you take that cubby-hole back there in the corner. He then disappeared, whistling, 'One More Drop for the Road.'

Kalle woke us at daybreak and asked my uncle if he knew how to drive a horse and buggy. The owner, Herr Volk, was moving out and needed someone to drive a cart loaded with feed bags.

Herr Volk showed up in person a little later. He was wearing a hunting hat, a loden coat and knickerbockers. And Frau Volk came to bestow a kind and cultured word on the women. I didn't like her because she called me by my first name without asking and allowed her dachshund bitch, Suzie, to sniff at our legs. Then the shooting began right behind us and we headed off at a quick pace. God takes care of his own, said my grandmother.

This is supposed to be a report on *liberation*, the hour of liberation, and I thought nothing could be easier. That hour has been clearly focused in my mind all these years; it has lain ready and waiting, fully completed in my memory. I need only say the word and the machine will start running, and everything will appear on the paper as if of its own accord—a series of accurate, highly defined pictures. But do they add up to anything?

I saw my first corpse at the age of sixteen; rather late for those years. (I don't count the infant I handed in a stiff bundle from a truck to a refugee woman; I didn't see him, I only heard his mother scream and run away.) Chance had it that Herr Volk's foreman, Wilhelm Grund, was lying dead instead of me, for pure chance alone had kept my uncle with a sick horse in the barn that morning, so that we weren't heading towards the country road alongside Grund's ox cart as usual. We could hear the gunfire from the barn, and the fifteen stabled horses were wild with fear. I have been afraid of horses ever since. But what I have feared more since that moment are the faces of people forced to see what no person should have to see. Wilhelm Grund's son, the young farmhand Gerhard Grund, had such a face as he burst through the barn door, managed a few steps and then collapsed: Herr Volk, what have they done to my father!

Gerhard was my age. His father lay in the dust at the side of the road next to his oxen, eyes staring upwards. Nothing would lower that gaze, not his wife's wailing or the whining of his three other children. This time around, they forgot to tell us that this was not a sight for us children.

'Quick,' said Herr Volk. 'We've got to get out of here.' They grabbed the corpse by the shoulders and legs and dragged him to the edge of the woods and wrapped him in the tarpaulins from the granary of the estate—just as they would have wrapped any of us, myself included. I, too, would have gone to the grave without words and without song—only their wailing—just like Wilhelm Grund the farmhand, and then they would have pushed on. For a long time they would have said nothing, just as we remained silent, and then would have had to ask what they needed to do now to stay alive. They would have torn off large birch branches, just as we did now, to cover the handcarts, as if the foreign pilots would be fooled by this little wandering birch grove. Everything, everything would be like now, only I would no longer be one of them. And the difference, which was everything to me, meant hardly anything to most of the others here. Gerhard Grund was already sitting in his father's seat, driving the oxen forward with his very whip, and Herr Volk nodded to him: 'Good boy. Your father died a soldier's death.'

I didn't really believe this. It wasn't the way a soldier's death had been described in the textbooks and newspapers, and I told that authority with whom I was continuously in touch and whom I labelled with the name of God—though against my own scruples and reservations—that, in my opinion, a man and father of four children did not deserve an end such as this.

I happened to be on guard at the time. It was my job to signal the next attacks by whistling. There were two American fighters. The birch grove came to a halt. Just as I had figured, it was clearly visible from afar and easy prey on the desolate country road.

Everything that had legs jumped out of the handcarts and threw itself in the ditch, myself included. This time I did not bury my head in the sand but lay on my back and continued eating my sandwich. I did not want to die and I certainly was not up to defying death but I did want to see the one who dared shoot at me. First I saw the white stars under the wings, and then the helmet-covered heads of the pilots and, finally, the naked white spots of their faces. I had seen prisoners before, but this was the attacking enemy—face to face. I knew that I was supposed to hate him and it seemed unnatural that I found myself wondering for the space of a second if they were having fun.

When we got back to the wagons, one of our oxen sank to its knees. Blood spurted from its throat. My uncle and grandfather unharnessed it. My grandfather, who had stood alongside the dead Wilhelm Grund without uttering a word, now hurled curses from his toothless mouth. 'The innocent creature,' he said hoarsely. 'Those damned bastards.' I was afraid he might begin to cry and hoped he would get everything off his chest by cursing. I forced myself to look at the animal for an entire minute. It couldn't be reproach that I detected in its gaze, so why did I feel guilty? Herr Volk handed his hunting rifle to my uncle and pointed to a spot behind the ox's ear. We were sent away. At the sound of the shot, I looked back. The ox dropped heavily on to its side.

All evening the women were busy cooking the meat. By the time we sat in the straw, sipping broth, it was already dark. Kalle, who had bitterly complained about being hungry, greedily slurped from his bowl, wiped his mouth on his sleeve and began to sing croakingly with contentment, 'All dogs bite, all dogs bite, but only hot dogs get bitten . . . '

'To hell with you, you crazy fellow,' my grandfather went at him furiously. Kalle fell on to the straw and stuck his head under his jacket.

One need not be afraid when everyone else is afraid. To know this is certainly liberating, but liberation was still to come, and I want to record what today's memory is prepared to yield on the subject. It was the morning of the 5 May, a beautiful day, and once more panic broke out when we heard that we were encircled by Soviet armoured tank troops. Then word came that we should march to Schwerin, where the Americans were. Anyone still capable of asking a question would have found it strange, that surge forward towards the enemy who had been trying to kill us for days now. But no one did. The world stubbornly refused to end and we were not prepared to cope with a world that refused to end. I remember the horrific words uttered by one woman when told that the miracle weapon longed for by the Führer could only exterminate everyone, both the enemy and the Germans. Let them go ahead and use it, she said.

We moved past the last houses of a village along a sandy road. A soldier was washing up at a pump next to a red Mecklenburg farmhouse. He stood there, legs apart, with the sleeves of his white undershirt rolled up, and called out to us, 'The Führer is dead,' the same way one says, 'Nice weather today.' I was stunned more at his tone than at the realization that the man was speaking the truth.

I trudged on alongside our cart, heard the coachmen's hoarse shouts, the groaning of the exhausted horses, saw the small fires by the side of the road where the papers of the officers of the Wehrmacht smouldered. There were heaps of guns and anti-tank grenade-launchers sprouting from the ditches, along with typewriters, suitcases, radios and all manner of precious war equipment senselessly lining our way.

Then came the paper. The road was suddenly flooded with paper; they were still throwing it out of the Wehrmacht vehicles in wild anger—forms, induction orders, files, proceedings, documents from the headquarters of a military district, banal routine letters as well as military secrets and the statistics of the dead. As if there were something repulsive about the paper trash, I did not stoop to pick up a page, which I regretted later. I did, however, catch the canned food which a truck driver threw to me. The swing of his arm reminded me of the movement, often performed, with which, in the summer of '39, I had thrown cigarette packs on to the dusty convoys which rolled eastward past our house, day and night. In the six-year interim I had stopped being a child; summer was coming again, but I had no idea how I would spend it.

The supply convoy of a Wehrmacht unit had been abandoned by its escort on a side road. All those who passed by took as much as they could carry. The order of the column dissolved. Many were beside themselves, no longer with fear but with greed. Only Kalle laughed, dragging a large block of butter to our cart, clapping his hands and shouting happily, 'Well, I'll be damned! Look at them getting all worked up!'

Then, out of nowhere, we saw the prisoners from the concentration camp nearby. They stood at the edge of the forest and gazed at us. We could have given them a sign that the air was clear, but nobody did. Cautiously, they approached the road. They looked different from all the people I had seen up to then, and I wasn't surprised that we automatically shrank back from them. But it betrayed us, this shrinking back; it showed that, in spite of what we protested to each other and ourselves, we knew. All we unhappy ones who had been driven away from all our possessions, from our farms and our manors, from our shops and musty bedrooms and brightly polished parlours with the picture of the Führer on the wall—we knew. These people, who had been declared animals and who were slowly coming towards us to take revenge—we had abandoned them. Now the ragged would put on our clothes and stick their bloody feet in our shoes, now the starved would seize hold of the flour and the sausage that we had snatched. And to my horror I felt that it was just, and I was horrified to feel that it was just, and knew for a fraction of a second that we were guilty. I forgot it again.

The prisoners pounced not on the bread but on the guns by the side of the road. They loaded up on ammunition, crossed the road without paying any attention to us, struggled up the opposite slope and mounted sentry there. They looked down at us. I couldn't bear looking at them. Why don't they scream, I thought, or shoot into the air, or shoot at us, goddamnit! But they stood there peacefully. Some of them were reeling and could barely bring themselves to hold their guns and stand up. Perhaps they had been praying for this moment. Everything about them was completely foreign to me.

There came a call from the front that everybody except the drivers should dismount. This was an order. A deep breath went through the convoy, for this could mean only one thing: the final steps towards freedom lay ahead. Before we could move on, the Polish drivers jumped off, coiled the reins around the stanchion of the wagon, formed a small squad and set about going back, eastward. Herr Volk, immediately turning a bluish-red colour, blocked their way. At first he spoke quietly to them, but soon he began to scream. Conspiracy, foul play, refusal to work, he shouted. A Polish migrant worker then pushed Herr Volk aside.

The world had truly turned topsy-turvy, only Herr Volk hadn't noticed yet; he reached for his whip, but it was stopped in mid-air; someone was holding his arm. The whip dropped to the ground, and the Poles walked on. His hand pressed against his heart, Herr Volk leaned heavily against the cart and let himself be comforted by his thin-lipped wife, while Kalle railed at him from above, shouting, Bastard, bastard. The French people, who stayed with us, called out farewells to the departing Poles, who understood those farewells no more than I did, but understood their sound. It hurt being so strictly excluded from their shouting, waving and the tossing of their caps, from their joy and their language. But it had to be that way. The world consisted of the victors and the vanquished. The former were free to express their emotions. We had to lock ours inside us. The enemy should not see us weak.

There he was. I would have preferred a fire-breathing dragon to this light Jeep with its gum-chewing driver and three casual officers. I tried to make an expressionless face and look right through them, and told myself that their unconstrained laughter, their clean uniforms, their indifferent glances, the whole damned victor's pose had probably been planned for our special humiliation.

The people around me began to hide watches and rings. I, too, took my watch off my wrist and carelessly put it in my coat pocket. The guard at the end of the line, a lanky, hulking man, showed the few people carrying arms where to throw their weapons, while he frisked us civilians with a few firm, routine police motions. Petrified with indignation but secretly proud that they believed me capable of carrying a weapon, I let myself be searched, and my overworked sentry routinely asked, 'Your watch?'

So he wanted my watch, the victor, but I told him that the other one, 'your comrade,' his brother officer, had already pocketed it.

It was then that my heightened sense of hearing signalled the rising sound of an airplane engine.

I kept an eye on its approach route out of habit and threw myself to the ground as it swooped down; once more the horrid dark shadow flitting quickly across grass and trees, once more the atrocious sound of bullets pounding into soil. Still? I thought to myself in astonishment, realizing that one can get used to the feeling of being out of danger in a second.

I should be capable of saying how it felt when it became quiet. I stayed put behind the tree. I believe the thought did not occur to me that, from now on, no bomb would be dropped on me again. I wasn't curious about what would happen next. I didn't know how the horned Siegfried is supposed to act if the dragon asks him for his watch rather than gobbling him up, hair and hide. I didn't feel like watching how Herr Siegfried and Herr Dragon would get along as private citizens. I didn't feel like going to the Americans in the occupied mansion for every bucket of water or having a fight with black-haired Lieutenant Davidson from Ohio.

And I felt less up to the talk with the concentration-camp prisoner who sat with us by the fire at night, wearing a pair of bent wire-frame spectacles and mentioning the word 'Communism' as if it were a permitted, household world such as 'hatred' or 'war' or 'extermination'. No. And least of all did I feel like knowing about the sadness and the dismay which were in his voice when he asked us, 'Where, then, have you lived all these years?'

I didn't feel up to liberation. I was lying under my tree; all was quiet. I was lost and wanted to make a note of the branches against that very beautiful May sky, when my lanky, off-duty sergeant came up the slope, a squealing German girl hanging on each arm. All three moved in the direction of the occupied mansion, and finally I had a reason to turn away a little and cry.

Translated from the German by Heike Schwarzbauer and
Rick Takvorian

GRANTA

IAN BURUMA
BUCHENWALD

Once upon a time, on top of a green hill, high above the red roofs of Weimar, there was an oak tree. So beautiful was this spot on the Ettersberg, with views all round of the rolling Thuringian countryside, that Goethe used to sit here with his friend Johann Peter Eckermann discussing literature and life. Eckermann noted down the master's words: 'Here one feels great and free.'

In 1937, when the forest was cleared to build a concentration camp, Goethe's oak was protected by a special act decreed by the Nazi government. A fence was built around it. The splendid tree survived until the last year of the war, when one side caught fire during an American bomb attack. The guards decided to have it felled. An inmate of the camp, who made death masks in the medical lab, used some of the wood to carve a human face which can still be seen in the museum of the 'Warning and Memorial Place Buchenwald' (*Mahn- und Gedenkstatte Buchenwald*).

The exact spot of Goethe's oak was pointed out to me in the winter of 1991, during my second visit to Buchenwald. My German guide was a tall thin man, whose ingratiating manner suggested nervousness. 'Here you can see,' he said, indicating the camp in one swooping gesture, 'the typical German mentality. The Goethe oak: culture and romanticism. The crematorium: barbarism. The zoo: sentimentality.'

I had not heard about the zoo before. Created to amuse the guards, it was located just outside the barbed wire fence, near the main gate (the animals, needless to say, were much better treated than Buchenwald's inmates). Otherwise, my guide's review of the German 'mentality' was a cliché.

But it was a cliché not often heard in Buchenwald itself, until recently. The Buchenwald concentration camp was, after all, the 'Red Olympus', the shrine of the East German Communists' anti-fascist struggle. Many of their most important leaders had been imprisoned here; Ernst Thälmann, the chairman of the Communist Party before the war, was murdered in Buchenwald. And an alleged last-minute uprising in April 1945, led by leftist prisoners,

Opposite: the monument at the entrance to Buchenwald, showing prisoners protecting their communist banner.

Photo: Associated Press

had entered communist lore as the event which had virtually founded the German Democratic Republic. That the German mentality was now being blamed for all that had happened in Buchenwald was a sign of how much had changed in the last two years.

On my first visit to Buchenwald, a year earlier, everything was still normal—that is to say, orthodox. Like most visitors from the West, I was struck and somewhat horrified by the grandiose monuments erected on the site of the mass graves. Along the Street of Nations were eighteen huge stone pylons, crowned by great chalices, representing the countries where the Nazis had rounded up their victims. There was the soaring, forty-five metre tower, whose bell, my guide book said, would 'echo through the land'. Inside the tower a bronze plate covered soil taken from various concentration camps. There was the outsized sculpture of heroic prisoners breaking their bonds and raising their fists in a salute to the future. There were friezes of still more heroic prisoners punishing their tormentors, or better yet, in the words of the Buchenwald Oath, taken on the day of liberation in April 1945, 'tearing out the Nazi evil by its roots.'

I saw the cell where Ernst Thälmann, the Stalinist hero, was killed. There were plaques, an eternal flame and wreaths from fraternal parties and trade union organizations.

But the myth of Buchenwald contained a hole in the middle. There was hardly any mention of the Jews who had died here of overwork, disease and hunger, in medical experiments and in executions. Of all the prisoners, the Jews had been treated worst. Yet I found only one small plaque to commemorate the 'special camp', where 10,000 German Jews had languished after the arrests of *Kristallnacht*. About the transports from Auschwitz of tens of thousands of Jews, many of whose skeletal remains had to be literally scraped from the cattle trucks, there was not a word.

In communist dogma, the war against the Jews did not really exist. World War Two had been a class war, waged by fascists and plutocrats against the People. Jews, then, were essentially no different from the other victims of fascism. As my guidebook, printed in 1988, put it: 'Destruction of Marxism, revenge for the lost war and brutal terror against all resisters, these were the stated aims of German fascism from the very start. These covered the interests of monopoly capital, which lavishly promoted the Nazi movement.'

The same guidebook did contain two photographs of the selection ramp at Auschwitz, where ninety per cent of the victims were Jewish. But the caption consisted only of a quote from Ernst Thälmann that 'the bourgeoisie is serious about its aim to annihilate the party and the entire avant garde of the working class.'

Like all concentration camp sites, Buchenwald attracts the usual combination of tourists (one of the barracks has been turned into a hotel), survivors and ghouls. I was accosted in the car park, just outside the notorious iron gate, decorated with the motto '*Jedem das Seine*' ('to each his own'), by an American veteran, who told me he visited the camp once a year. He claimed to have been with General Patton's leathernecks, who liberated the camp on 11 April 1945. 'The ovens were still warm,' he drawled.

This version of events does not quite fit the orthodoxy. The Communist myth of Buchenwald has it that the inmates, led by a resistance organization inside the camp, liberated themselves in a heroic uprising. There was indeed a resistance group in the camp, and its members did capture some weapons. But whether these weapons were ever used is open to question. Several survivors have claimed that the camp was liberated—without bloodshed—by the American Army. As Patton's tanks surrounded the camp, the guards either fled or surrendered. This version has the ring of truth: it is hard to imagine how an uprising led by a group of hungry, emaciated, exhausted men could have succeeded without the Allies on hand.

Even so, the Buchenwald uprising is important because it is in effect the founding myth of the German Democratic Republic. Every East German schoolchild had to read *Naked amongst the Wolves*, by Bruno Apitz, the man who carved a face mask out of Goethe's oak. It is a clumsy novel of the socialist realist school, in which the men of the communist resistance committee contrive, at great danger to themselves, to save a little Jewish boy, while

69

plotting the final uprising. The book revolves round the question of collective versus individual interests. Is the life of one individual worth jeopardizing in the interests of the community? It is never quite resolved. In the event, both boy and community are saved. During the final, climactic scene, the heroes press through the main camp gate and 'drag along on the crests of their liberating waves the unstoppable stream of humanity.'

And so began, in the words of the Buchenwald Oath (sworn on the parade ground that very same day) the struggle 'towards a new world of peace and freedom.' The nature of this new socialist world soon became clear. When Otto Grotewohl, the first prime minister of the German Democratic Republic, addressed 80,000 people at a rally in the former Buchenwald camp in 1958, he declared that the Oath had already come true in East Germany. To pay tribute to this achievement, hundreds of thousands of schoolchildren, workers, socialist youths, soldiers, farmers and foreign comrades flocked every year to the 'Red Olympus' to lay wreaths, listen to speeches, march in torchlight parades and generally demonstrate their resolve to continue on the road to the communist millenium.

But by 1991, when I visited Buchenwald for the second time, things had begun to change. The grandiose monuments were still there, of course. So was the documentary film shown in the movie theatre, which contained footage of Otto Grotewohl, Walter Ulbricht and Mrs Thälmann marching along the Street of Nations. But I was also handed a new pamphlet which announced, with excruciating delicacy, that it had been decided in the spring of 1990 to 'institute some changes, as far as technically feasible, to overcome a certain one-sidedness in the presentation.'

These words convey nothing of the controversy involved in rewriting the myths of the German Democratic Republic. Rewriting myths on a historical site, a 'warning and memorial place' so loaded with symbolism, is full of pitfalls. The main difficulty is to challenge old myths without simply replacing them with new ones. The holy shrine of Buchenwald is particularly problematic, since one or two skeletons have tumbled from its cupboards.

In 1983, builders came across a mass of human bones, dumped into a common grave in the woods outside the perimeters of the

Nazi camp. The East German government immediately ordered the grave, and the matter, closed. But after 1989, more bones were discovered. What could not be mentioned for forty years was now openly discussed: Buchenwald, along with other concentration camps in East Germany, such as Sachsenhausen and Ravensbrück, had remained fully operative until 1950. As soon as the Soviet army arrived in Weimar, they pressed Buchenwald back into service: this time to punish former Nazis, class enemies and counter-revolutionaries, including social democrats who refused to let the communists take over their party. There is no evidence that the Russians subjected their prisoners to the Nazi regime of murder by hard labour, medical experiments and execution. Still, one-third of the 30,000 prisoners who were interned in Soviet Buchenwald died, mostly of hunger and disease.

I met one of the survivors in west Berlin. Robert Zeiler's story, which he has told for years—to students, journalists, survivors' associations—is a kind of epic myth in itself. Zeiler's father was a gentile orchestra conductor; his mother was Jewish. When Zeiler was eleven, the first racial laws were passed; shortly afterwards, his parents were divorced. Still, thanks to the 'leniency' of the new laws, the half-gentile Zeiler could protect his mother by living under her roof.

By 1943, the Nazi regime had decided that no Jew was to be spared. Zeiler's mother was picked up and sent to a concentration camp near Prague. Soon after, Zeiler, now twenty, was arrested for harbouring Jews—that is to say, his own mother. He was sent to Buchenwald. Before long, he weighed only ninety pounds.

After being liberated by Patton's troops, Zeiler went to Czechoslovakia in an American jeep to find his mother. Together, they drove to Potsdam. When Zeiler decided to take the jeep on to Berlin, he was arrested by the Soviet secret police, who accused him of being an American spy. Zeiler insisted that he was a Jewish victim of the Nazis, but was told that he was a liar; all Jews were dead. After some months of being shunted from one camp to another, he found himself in Buchenwald once more. There he spent the next three years. The guards, he recalled, were not brutes; they were mostly homesick young men, who liked singing sentimental songs. The worst thing about the Soviet camp, Zeiler said, was the boredom.

I asked Zeiler what people thought of his story when he finally got back to Berlin. He studied the tea cloth on his table, which had a picture of the Hiroshima Peace Dome embroidered on it. He had told his story to many people, he said, to the Germans as well as the occupation authorities. Then he fell silent. I studied his room, filled with knick-knacks and his father's musical mementoes. Again I asked how people had responded to the stories about Soviet Buchenwald. He said that nobody had showed any interest at the time. Everyone was still preoccupied by the Nazis. In the German Democratic Republic, the subject of the Russian camps simply did not exist.

Dr Irmgard Seidel was still the deputy director of the memorial place Buchenwald when I visited the camp for the second time. Her office was in one of the former SS barracks. It was a large building, with long corridors, built by prisoners; inside, it smelled of wax and washing detergent. On the wall, next to the door of Dr Seidel's office, was a drawing of an SS man, whip in hand, standing in front of a torture victim who hung from a pole by his wrists. In the caption, the victim said: 'Lord, forgive him, for he knows not what he does.'

'I had no idea about this Soviet camp,' said Dr Seidel, when I asked her about it. 'December 1989 was the first time I heard about it. You know, what happened here between 1945 and 1950 was a taboo. It could not possibly be discussed.'

Dr Seidel's manner was not exactly impolite, but it was brusque and betrayed a great deal of resentment. A former Party member, Seidel now lived in a new Germany unified under conservative Christian Democrats. The tables had truly turned: a committee of concerned Weimar citizens was agitating to have her removed from her job. Dr Seidel's boss had already been purged, only to be replaced by a West German historian, who was also swiftly removed when his connections with the West German

Opposite: a British delegation of MPs visiting Buchenwald, 1945.

Photo: Hulton Deutsch Collection

Communist Party became known. His place was taken by another young West German, who had no communist connections, so far as anyone knew.

Dr Seidel was eager to show me documents proving her bona fides, and in particular her independence from communist propaganda. She was especially conscious of the way the socialist state had ignored the Holocaust. To prove that she now had the right kind of backing, she produced a letter from a society of Holocaust survivors in New York. It was a protest against any attempt to equate the victims of the Soviets to the Nazi victims. The letter also praised the bravery of German political prisoners, 'whose sacrifices laid the foundation of the moral rebirth of Germany.' 'Of course,' said Dr Seidel. 'we have neglected the Jewish victims, but this we intend to change. Our Jewish friends know this and support me fully.'

Perhaps they do, and maybe Dr Seidel had reason to feel maligned. Still, I couldn't quite believe all of her protestations. She must have known something, for instance, about the postwar history of the camp. A booklet, printed in Weimar in 1988, and freely available at the camp museum bookshop, mentioned the kind co-operation of the Soviet authorities in turning Buchenwald into a memorial place. This was made possible, it said, in 1950, when 'the internment camp for Nazi functionaries was cleared in four weeks.'

But what is to be done, now the the truth—or at least some of the truth—is known? German conservatives are quick to point out the similarities between Soviet and Nazi crimes. 'It is time,' wrote a contributor to the *Frankfurter Allgemeine Zeitung*, 'to dust off the totalitarianism theory once more: the idea that right-wing and left-wing tyrannies may not be identical, but should be assessed in the same way. What better place for this theory to prove its worth than Buchenwald?' The Christian Democratic Party in Weimar wants to turn the camp into a 'memorial place for the victims of all dictatorships'—as though the Third Reich were just another dictatorship.

Buchenwald, then has become the handy focus of a view which has gained currency, particularly in right-wing circles, since the collapse of the German Democratic Republic: that the communist state was a kind of continuation of the Third Reich. The Stasi, conservatives currently argue, was actually much more pervasive—and more efficient—than the Gestapo. In a way, it is argued, the German Democratic Republic was even worse than Nazi Germany: it lasted for more than forty years, whereas Hitler was only around for twelve.

It's an attractive theory, since it reduces the Third Reich to more local, less horrific proportions. It also slides easily into the conclusion that started the historians' debate, or *Historikerstreit*, in 1986: the conclusion that Nazism was merely a defensive reaction to Soviet aggression. And the historians' debate came only one year after Chancellor Helmut Kohl's invitation to Ronald Reagan to stand hand in hand at the cemetery in Bitburg. In a great moment of reconciliation, Kohl thought, it would be churlish, indeed it would be missing the point entirely, to distinguish between the graves of SS men and other victims of war. The idea was that all had been victims of history. The time had come to forget about distinctions. To paraphrase the historian Ernst Nolte, it was time for the past to go away.

But it won't go away, especially in what used to be the German Democratic Republic. Just a few months ago, on the eve of the Jewish New Year, neo-Nazi vandals burnt down a barrack in the former concentration camp of Sachsenhausen, in an eastern suburb of Berlin. It had been a special barrack for Jews. German papers condemned the act as an anti-Semitic attack which would darken Germany's name abroad. But it was more than that. It was also an assault on contemporary Germany, on the rich West, on the decrepit East, on fifty years of tyranny and lies. East Germans were forced to believe in myths, and now they are left with nothing. It was horribly apt that the outrage should have happened in the middle of a place of remembrance.

SACRED HUNGER

BARRY UNSWORTH

WINNER OF THE 1992 BOOKER PRIZE

'It carries the reader deep into the history of man's iniquitous greed . . . As regards its dramatic breadth and energy, no recent domestic novel has come within a mile of it'

- ANTHONY QUINN IN THE INDEPENDENT

'Vivid, realistic, frequently surprising, full of incident, exciting and terrible by turns. The result is an irresistible novel of action, such as one rarely meets today . . . Read it, whatever other novels you fail to read this year'

- ALLAN MASSIE IN THE SCOTSMAN

'A magnificent novel'
- MARGARET FORSTER IN THE SUNDAY TELEGRAPH

OUT IN PAPERBACK

GRANTA

DORIS DÖRRIE
LOVE IN GERMANY

Doris Dörrie: Does a married couple have to be faithful?

Ottilie: Yes, not necessarily these days, I don't know. It's certainly nice if you're faithful—like we used to be. Whatever you do you don't discu . . . disc . . . think about it all the time and what somebody's done wrong and so on, you have to forget about it. Do you understand? Just put it out of your mind.

Rudolph: There's always a bit of a crisis, basically.

Ottilie: My husband had a girlfriend and—I didn't care, mind you—I just thought, if *you* can do it . . .

Rudolph: You don't have to say all this.

Ottilie: Oh, it's just talk. A doctor told me that there are no faithful men.

Doris Dörrie: Wasn't it very painful?

Ottilie: At the beginning, of course it was! Because I was so trusting. But now I think every marriage has to go through that at some point. We didn't split up.

Doris Dörrie: Can you remember why you started a relationship with the other woman?

Rudolph: Yes, I sort of chopped this woman's wood for her, didn't I? She was a widow and I was always chopping her wood because, well, why not? It was a bit of extra money. She had a good pension. She needed a bit of—she needed some love, to put it bluntly. You see . . .

All kinds of generalizations have been made about the German 'character'. But what kind of generalizations can we make about the Germans in love? Last year film-maker and writer Doris Dörrie spent several months interviewing German couples about their love-lives. We include a selection.

Opposite: Ottilie, housewife, and Rudolph, forestry worker.

Doris Dörrie: And did you consider that it might hurt your wife?

Ottilie: No, I don't think he did! So I thought, anything you can do, I can do better. That was my revenge. He thought I wouldn't get anybody, and he was wrong.

Doris Dörrie: And how did you meet him?

Ottilie: Him? He was always driving past and waving and honking his horn and peering into the house—he drove by more and more slowly, and then one day he spoke to me: he wanted a date—he spent four years persuading me. Four years! And then we had a love affair for two years and then I left him, I didn't want any more. I could have the same man today, he's divorced. He'd like to have me again now.

Doris Dörrie: So how come you got back together again at the end of these two affairs?

Ottilie: So people wouldn't talk and because of the children and, Frau Dörrie, I'll even say this to you, you're married, like me: I think that a thing like this really strengthens a marriage, when you go through something. My husband could have left me and I could have left him, you see?

Doris Dörrie: But it's terribly painful, isn't it?

Ottilie: Madly painful.

Rudolph: Well . . .

Ottilie: It was madly painful for me.

Rudolph: Of course. What I'd say, for myself, basically, it wasn't a love affair at all, to put it bluntly.

Ottilie: It was for me.

Rudolph: In practice . . .

Ottilie: It was for me.

Rudolph: She was an old woman. Over sixty-five, she was over sixty-five, wasn't she? Because she'd never got any love from her husband. He liked a drink.

Doris Dörrie: What did you find with her?

Rudolph: Companionship, frankly.

Ottilie: Well! I didn't see any companionship there!

Rudolph: You think I did it for love? It was mostly for money.

Ottilie: I didn't have to buy it. He didn't have to give me any money.

Rudolph: She gave me a nice bit of veal, one time.

Ottilie: No, he didn't have to give me any money. Ours was real love, real true love.

Rudolph: I'm sure.

Doris Dörrie: Aren't you at all jealous?

Rudolph: No, not me, really not. I'm fond of her, my wife, really, I'd be lying, but I say it all the time: I'm fond of my wife, but if someone else likes her better he should take her. It's an old saying. You see, there wouldn't be anything I could do about it then, would there?

Doris Dörrie: The dating agency for fat people put me in touch with you. Tell me why you applied to it?

Stefan: Well, I've been looking for a partner for a long time, but I can't find one because of my weight.

Doris Dörrie: Has anything come of it?

Stefan: I was matched up with someone. She's stout as well, if you like, and a big Wagner fan, as I am. But it didn't work. We both decided, or rather the lady decided, that she found me too—although she finds me very pleasant company—that I'm, somehow, *too* stout. So basically it wouldn't be possible for her to live with me.

Doris Dörrie: Have you ever had a partner?

Stefan: Once, but after a brief affair—if I might put it like that—she left me. The whole thing turned out to be just a big lie. I gave her my money, the little bit I had, and she made all kinds of promises—then she disappeared with the lot.

Doris Dörrie: Was this lady stout as well, as you say?

Stefan: No, she was as slim as can be.

Doris Dörrie: And was it a sexual relationship?

Stefan: Yes, it was. After she'd left I wouldn't let anyone speak to me. I didn't dare go out in case she rang. We planned to get married, you see. It had been—from my point of view—love at first sight. But I fell back to earth very quickly after that. My mother was a great help. Because I was so depressed she brought me a pet, a guinea pig.

Doris Dörrie: Did you swear never to fall in love again?

Stefan: On the contrary, I started looking immediately. I tried everything I could think of. I took out personal ads and answered them; but I never actually got a reply.

This winter I went to Thailand with my mother, and it was fantastically beautiful! I went on outings, or just lazed around on the beach or the swimming pool. I had two nicknames: either '*bumbui*' or 'sexy man'. *Bumbui* means strong man. Weight isn't seen so negatively down there; they believe in Buddha. And although there are actually two different Buddhas, the Thai Buddha, who's pretty slim, and the Chinese Buddha—who's basically exactly the same as me, very corpulent—they look at you very differently there. They literally run after you. They come running after you from all directions.

Doris Dörrie: The women?

Stefan: Some of them came flying at me, so to speak.

Opposite: Stefan, travel agent.

Doris Dörrie: And did you have a girlfriend?

Stefan: Yes, I met her in a bar, and then I spent every day with her for three weeks. She slept in my room.

Doris Dörrie: And was that love?

Stefan: Well, it is true that they're professionals over there, but that doesn't mean the same as it does here. I think the two of us got on very well. I got some very nice cards—'I love you,' and stuff like that. I mean you don't write things like that for a laugh.

I'd like to have brought her back, but you have to give them a one-year return flight, and that costs money. It's true that you can bring them back with the charter companies without any problems, in fact, I met a fair number of people who brought one back on one of those planes. The girls turned up at the airport with all their belongings. I simply didn't have the money, but I'd like to fly back there if I have the chance.

Valentin: Yes—passion . . .

Erika: Ooooh, it can only arise out of love. For me the husband must conquer the wife—must be allowed to—because a woman wants to be conquered, and then, then what happens is that . . .

Valentin: I'm your conqueror then?

Erika: Ooooh!—and then comes the nice bit.

Doris Dörrie: How important is sex?

Valentin: I think it's great the way we've got it.

Erika: He didn't really know much before—

Valentin: It's a new feeling for me.

Erika: After eighteen years of marriage.

Valentin: That's true. When I compare my marriage to the last

Opposite: Erika, ex-artiste, and Valentin, bank clerk.

few years, I can see that it was just routine.

Erika: Exactly. It happened—OK, fine—but you didn't know anything was missing. Whereas we have only to talk on the phone and I get the feeling. It only happens with him, nobody else. He's the man. All this here [she tugs at his hair] is my doing. The hair he had when I met him made him look like a forty-five year old.

Doris Dörrie: What did you do with him?

Valentin: She remodelled me.

Erika: He'd had bad luck, two teeth out. The first thing I said to him was, Darling, get your teeth done. The very first thing.

Valentin: I had two gold teeth, it bothered me.

Erika: Everyone said: What's up with your boyfriend? How come he has no teeth? I couldn't believe his family let him walk around like that. Not that it bothered me—I like his little mouth [flicks at his lips]. And then his straight hair! I said, Darling, go to the Italian hairdresser, get a haircut. People asked if it was a wig. And then those skiing jumpers! All knitted by mums or grannies—couldn't have that. I styled him, as they say; gave him a leather jacket and everything.

Doris Dörrie: So how do you imagine your future?

Yvonne: More than anything I'd like to get married, have children, maybe two or even three. But at some point I'd also like to have my own business.

Franz: Well, I'm a great dreamer, always have been. I've always imagined things going as follows: girlfriend. Job. Marriage. Children. If I imagine her getting pregnant now, with her still in training and me still to establish a professional career—then we'd be in dreadful trouble.

Opposite: Franz, dance-teacher, and Yvonne, trainee dance-teacher.

Doris Dörrie: What does love mean to you?

Franz: Being on the same wavelength: the one that says, we belong together. Of course, you always have desires, you always have new goals and ideas, and perhaps for that reason you're more quickly dissatisfied, because we're born into this kind of luxury, where you have everything, where you can get everything.

Yvonne: I think I've had a very good example to follow: I mean my parents. They have a very harmonious relationship. It's a very important thing for me that somebody's always there for me, not just for fun—but also if I'm having a bad time.

Doris Dörrie: Do you ever need relationships with other people?

Franz: I couldn't imagine sleeping with another woman, just having a one-night stand.

Doris Dörrie: The sexual revolution is completely over?

Yvonne: I have a stable partner; I don't think it's worth worrying about.

Doris Dörrie: Fidelity?

Yvonne and **Franz**: Yes.

Doris Dörrie: So how important is sex for a relationship?

Franz: Sex just happens. It shouldn't be a duty. I must be able to say, 'I really fancy you now,' and then it happens or it doesn't. She must be able to say, 'OK then,' or 'I don't feel like it.' That's how it is with us—it suddenly happens anywhere.

Herr Müller: One girlfriend of mine was the same size as me, but we split up. When I went into our local on my own, an acquaintance asked me where she was. 'We split up,' I said, and didn't go into any more detail. Then came the

Opposite: Herr Müller, clerical worker, Andrea, office trainee, and Sabine, student.

prompt reply, 'But why? You suited each other so well.' What he meant was, you're the same size, why should you split up? Or the same thing, when I go shopping in town with Sabine or Andrea for instance, people automatically think we're a couple.

Andrea: I want my partner to accept me as I am. Everyone wants to hear sweet nothings, that's obvious. What's most important is that he should be willing to go around with me in public.

Sabine: I'd like to be able to rely on him on the one hand, but also to keep my own personality on the other.

Herr Müller: I used to travel a lot with my job, with big people, and I had—put it this way—'jester's licence' with the ladies. Which isn't to say that I could do anything I wanted, but I could do a bit more than everyone else, and when I think back I know why. It went more or less like this: ah, he's small and sweet—I'll let him do that, he's not doing much. Of course in a situation like that you can fall in love very quickly, and that happened many times. And when the lady noticed, that was it. Finished in that not only was the jester's licence out the window, but the lady wouldn't have anything more to do with me. She couldn't imagine a relationship coming out of it.

Sabine: Big people are usually inhibited and shy, so we always have to take the first step. We put them more at ease if we go up to them and talk to them quite normally, so to speak. Many of them are completely taken aback when they realize that being small doesn't mean being childlike, that we have a normal vocabulary.

Doris Dörrie: Doesn't it make you furious sometimes? That you always have to take the first step?

Sabine: No. It's the only situation I know.

Doris Dörrie: Do you dream of the big romance?

Andrea: Yes, yes, of course. Yes. [Laughter]

Herr Müller: On the other hand I've got used to the idea of maybe ending up alone when I'm a pensioner, but if I found a partner—why not? I have absolutely no objections to that. Going through life in a couple is much nicer, much more interesting than doing it alone. I have the opportunity for promotion at work, and I'd like to commit myself to that, but if I find the dream woman I won't say no.

Günter: We went to Freising, and I said, what do you say we get engaged next weekend? Just like that.

Sabine: No, it wasn't like that. It was just before Eching. You said, just in passing, what would you say to us getting engaged? Like that. I just sat there.

Günter: She kept her mouth shut for ten kilometres.

Sabine: I was speechless as far as Freising. I hadn't been expecting anything like that, not after such a short time.

Doris Dörrie: And what happened after that?

Sabine: We're both family types, we don't like being alone.

Günter: That's right, we're very affectionate.

Sabine: [Laughs] And I just enjoyed the fact that he could cook and knew something about housekeeping and so on.

Doris Dörrie: And love?

Günter: That's when you have mutual trust so that if one of you has troubles, they can confide in the other without keeping anything hidden. Many married couples can't do that. I would say that in Germany certainly fifty per cent of couples only exist on paper. I've tried to patch other marriages together; my own marriage collapsed, the first one.

Doris Dörrie: Why did it collapse?

Günter: My wife's alcoholism. She started drinking for some inexplicable reason. Nobody knows why, even now. It was everybody's fault but hers. I'd have stood by her, I'd have said,

go and dry out for two years. Then I said, I can't spend twelve hours in the bakery, be in charge of fourteen people and look after the children. I might not have divorced my wife if she'd gone on a drying-out cure. Eventually you reach the final straw. After that there were three other girlfriends, all a disappointment! One of them took my car, drove to her old boyfriend's and screwed him—in the car. The other one was only interested in money; I lost ten thousand marks. The third even got divorced for me, and then all this nonsense started: I had no time for her, she said. I'd told her what was what beforehand: that I had to keep the business going to pay maintenance for the kids. And all of a sudden she wanted to live it up, come and go when she wanted. Madam would come home in the evening for her dinner, and at eight she'd go off to live it up. They had sex orgies at Lake Heimstatt. I know all about it. It became a psychological torment for me. I knocked down three men and I stabbed her. I was put inside for a night.

Doris Dörrie: When did that happen?

Günter: They lay in wait for me, she and her boyfriends. They wanted to beat me half to death, and as I'm not exactly a six-stone weakling I gave them a good thrashing.

Doris Dörrie: Three?

Günter: She ran on to my knife. Half an inch deeper and she'd have been dead. Then I cracked up and they put me inside for a night. I totally cracked up. Of course I did, it's understandable. I know it was a mistake. I'm usually a quiet, sensible man. But I loved the woman! I imagined having a child with her. When I like a person I like them either all the way or not at all. I'd just like to say that there aren't just cruel men in the world, there are also very cruel women who can make life really hard for a man.

Opposite: Sabine, administrator, and Günter, baker.

Jürgen: It started when we were training. If you're training with heavy weights you need a partner to support you a bit. And it went nice and slowly from there.

Doris Dörrie: What was the first thing you liked about her?

Jürgen: That she trained, and that she had a good figure. It's like that in the fitness centre, everyone looks up when a new woman arrives. Everyone looks her up and down to see if she's any good, as they say. A good figure is one without much fat on it or skin like an orange.

Ellen: Cellulite, you mean.

Jürgen: The fact that she was fit, just the fact that she was doing something for her body.

Ellen: What struck me was that he isn't that big [laughter], and that he was always so calm. He just got on with his training and was never distracted. That was it, really.

Doris Dörrie: Your relationship is closely connected to your hobby?

Jürgen: Yes, absolutely. It's important first of all that I look good, and it's also important to me that she looks good, because then I get something out of it.

Ellen: More fun.

Jürgen: We do almost everything together: shopping, cleaning, washing up. We get up at half-past five in the morning. Then we mix up some quark: five hundred grams with half a litre of milk and then we put in this powder . . . And then we drink it. Because the body can only utilize about thirty grams of protein at once. Between half-past seven and eight o'clock I eat muesli for breakfast at work, and then at ten there's more quark. Depending on how we look we might eat a bit more. But if we're too fat we have to eat even less.

Opposite: Jürgen, butcher, and Ellen, civil servant.

Doris Dörrie: So what do you do when you come home from work?

Ellen: First of all we gulp down some amino acids and then we think about what we might eat. Then we cook a bit, and then we actually eat.

Doris Dörrie: You devote yourselves to your bodies so much. Do you find yourselves thinking that they're—slowly—decaying?

Ellen: When you train, your skin stays firm. That's how I see it. Only the day before yesterday we were watching a video and there was somebody wrestling who's almost sixty. He has the skin of a thirty-year-old or a forty-year-old. In the paper there's an American woman who's over sixty, and she looks good, really thin and fit, only using little weights, of course, but she looks great.

Jürgen: I'm not afraid of old age, it's a perfectly normal process, it happens to everybody.

Ellen: I often imagine what it'll be like when he's lost his hair, or when maybe he has grey hair. But I'll cope when it happens. He hates to see people who are closer to crawling than walking, and sometimes he'll comment and I have to say: careful, you don't know what you'll look like when you're old.

Doris Dörrie: What's happiness for you? What do you need?

Jürgen: We need our weights.

Ellen: Good weather.

Jürgen: Yes, and a bit of money. We don't need much. We know we love each other, and that's the most important thing. We both know that.

Translated from the German by Shaun Whiteside

GÜNTER GRASS
LOSSES

In the summer, my wife and I visited the small Danish island of Møn. We have been going there for years and by now have learned that to travel such a small distance offers no real escape from the news, particularly in the crisis month of August. The previous year the attempted coup in the disintegrating Soviet Union kept us huddled round the radio; the year before it was blanket coverage of the Gulf crisis; this year it was Germany.

The island of Møn has plenty to offer. It is a stopping-off place for a thousand and more grey geese, and in August there is heavy air traffic on the wide grazing pastures sheltered by Baltic dunes. All day long the geese practise take-off and landing. Sometimes herons will suddenly plunge and scatter them: wild consternation that gradually abates. The sky above the dunes and sea is always full of their formations.

Last August, though, the sky was empty but for a few seagulls. The dry summer had parched the grazing grounds, and there were no geese on the great airfields. Only the crises still arrived punctually by wireless. Two events arrived together, the sporting successes and failures of Barcelona and the war in Bosnia. The news overlapped. Events happening at the same time became the same events. The Olympic Games were being held in Sarajevo; the stadium was within reach of Serbian artillery. Here they totted up medals, there it was casualties. Terror became an Olympic discipline. A younger writer than me, with a lighter touch, would have found words to cover both arenas in one epic narrative: snipers and Ladies' Epée, beta blockers and blockade runners, abridged national anthems and the seventeenth pointless ceasefire, one lot of fireworks here, another there . . .

But all I noted down were thoughts about Germany. My confounded leaden-footedness! On our grey-goose island, we tried to avoid the disruptions of the crisis month; after all, blackberries abounded and there was fresh fish every day. But even between the chopped-off flounder heads—wrapped in yesterday's newspaper—there was room for small print and scraps of headlines.

Opposite: The funeral for Ayshe Yilmaz, aged fifty-one, Bahide Arslan, aged fourteen and Yeliz Arslan, aged ten, the female Turkish immigrants murdered in Mölln on 13 November 1992, to whom Günter Grass has dedicated this essay.

99

What is it that desensitizes sensitive people? We were irritable, but also dulled. Too much was happening at once. Can we blame the surfeit of information for our apathetic society: one person stares at the hole in the ozone layer, another harps on about the cost of health insurance. Spend too long wailing about the misery of the Bosnian refugees, and you forget to think about Somalia where people starve every day. Is the world out of joint or is it only the stock market going crazy again?

When the Games were over, Sarajevo had the headlines all to itself for a while, until even that nightmare no longer frightened us. Then came news from Germany, and we knew it was truly August.

In a way, it was nothing new, just the old story again. Over five hundred right-wing extremists repeatedly stormed a refugee hostel in Rostock-Lichtenhagen. From nearby windows, the citizenry looked on and applauded as stones and Molotov cocktails hit their targets. The police respected the display of popular will and kept well back. Shortly afterwards, they enthusiastically set off to arrest left-wing counter-demonstrators: to avoid possible escalation, as they said. On our radio we heard the politicians vying with one another in their well-rehearsed expressions of dismay.

But then more and more people watched the refugee hostels burning. The chanting was filmed and syndicated abroad. The 'ugly face of Germany' was rediscovered. There were no distractions this time, not the Olympics, not Kabul, not Sarajevo. ROSTOCK it said in big letters wherever you looked. And on my holiday island in Denmark—a country not overly fond of foreigners, but a place where recourse to the murderous hatred of Rostock is barely imaginable—I jotted down some questions: Is there no end to German recidivism? Do Germans necessarily botch everything, even the unification that was handed to us on a plate? Are we condemned to relive our history? Are we, even now, incapable of humane treatment of one another? What do we lack, with all our wealth?

Since Rostock, Germany has changed. We now know that all the assurances of those unification-happy days were hollow. The newspapers trumpeted the end of the post-war era, the beginning of a new chapter in our history—a dozen eager historians stood by to write it. But now all the repugnant triumphalist din has stopped, and the past has tapped us on the shoulder.

Not that the shock of being collared silenced us quite. There have been protests, demonstrations to prove our capacity to fight back; but the politics responsible for our lapse into barbarism over the last three years have remained on course: the individual right to asylum—the jewel of our constitution!—continues to be sacrificed to the god of popular feeling; the process of unification without unity accelerates; and neither government nor opposition is willing or able to call a halt to the shameless auctioning-off of the bankrupt GDR and think about how the burden might be shared.

The unfairness of that apportioning of the load has repeatedly driven me to speak out. For forty years the second-class citizens of the GDR, exploited, walled in, spied on and spoken for, have had to pay for the War on behalf of the whole of Germany. Bad luck they didn't make it to the west and freedom. Rather than acknowledging our debt, we in the west gave them more big-brothering. On 18 December 1989, at the Social Democrats' Party Congress in Berlin, I called for 'a complete programme of burden-sharing, to begin immediately and without further preconditions.' It should, I suggested, be financed out of arms cuts and a special graded income tax; but my comrades still preferred to believe in Willy Brandt's attractive phrase, 'what belongs together will grow together', even though it was clear, not many weeks after the collapse of the Wall, that not a lot was growing except a great many undesirable weeds. After forty years apart, all that we Germans have in common is the burden of a guilty past; even our language now divides us.

My speech about burden-sharing was quickly buried under a perfunctory round of applause. Since then, I have been a voice in the wilderness. On 2 February 1990, at a conference in Tutzing addressing 'New Answers to the German Question,' I argued that 'Whoever thinks about Germany now, and seeks answers for the German question, must include Auschwitz in his thoughts.'

That sentence, and further reflections of mine, warning against an over-hasty German unification and proposing a confederal structure for the two states, provoked a furore. I, the 'self-proclaimed gloom-merchant of the nation' and 'notorious enemy of Germany unity,' had, I was told, tried to use Auschwitz to restrict the German right to self-determination.

I should like to know if my unification-drunk critics of the time thought the same when the so-called 'Jewish barracks' in Sachsenhausen were burned to the ground? Or now that gypsies —nearly half a million Romany and Sinti people were murdered at Auschwitz and Auschwitz-Birkenau—are once again subjected to violence in Germany? Those critics—all of them parroting the silly stationmaster's line, 'The train has left the station'—should have considered where their metaphorical train would terminate.

The time for warnings is long past. And yet still there is no political force willing or able to prevent this new wave of crimes. Far from it: it wasn't the skinheads who first broke the democratic consensus. The recent agreement by Interior Minister Seiters with the Romanian government that provides for the repatriation of gypsies, and the stream of attacks on the asylum article in the constitution, are merely more elaborate versions of the slogan that presently unites all Germany: 'Foreigners out!'

The Federal Republic and its constitution have been handed over to the tender mercies of a demolition company. When a Christian Democratic politician, a finance minister no less, ventures a look into the future from under his shaggy brows and proclaims that future elections can only be won right of centre; when the Free Democrats borrow a brownish-shirted populist Austrian to address their meetings; when the minister representing the arms lobby proposes to go to Peenemünde to celebrate the golden anniversary of the V2 rocket—and it takes protests from abroad to dissuade him; and when this whole slide to the right is dismissed as tap-room chatter—then it's time we Germans recognized the threat we pose once more, preferably before our neighbours do.

Opposite: Romanies and Sinti living on a garbage dump near Stettin in Poland, waiting to cross the border to Germany.

As I mentioned, in this hard, dry summer, the geese had stopped flying to our holiday island. I had no distractions. The bitter lees of two years of unity finally leaked out on to paper. My Danish notes insist that I speak personally, of Germany and myself. How I didn't want to let go of the country. How it slipped from my grasp. What I miss. What I don't. My *losses*.

I noted a long line of losses, which I will cut to a few representative examples. The first of them is the loss of my homeland. But that loss, painful though it was, was also justified. German culpability for the criminal conduct of the war, the genocide of Jews and gypsies, the murder of millions of prisoners of war and forced labourers, the crime of euthanasia, the sufferings we brought to our neighbours, especially the Polish people, when we occupied their countries, all that led to the loss of my homeland.

Compared to millions of refugees faced with the difficulties of settling in the west, I had a relatively easy time of it. Language didn't compensate me for my loss, but by stringing words together I was able to make something in which my loss could be declared.

Most of my books invoke the old city of Danzig, its flat and hilly surroundings and the dull pulse of the Baltic; and with the years, Gdańsk, too, has become a subject for me. Loss has given me a voice. Only what is entirely lost demands to be endlessly named: there is a mania to call the lost thing until it returns. Without loss there would be no literature. (I could almost market that as a thesis.)

Furthermore, the loss of my homeland has offered me the opportunity of new loyalties. If you have a home, you tend to want to stay in it; but I am curious about the world and take delight in travelling. People without a homeland have broader horizons than those who live where their fathers and forefathers did. I needed no crutch of nationalism to feel myself to be German: I had my loss.

Other values became important to me. Their loss is harder to bear because the gaps they left can't be filled. I am used to being controversial in what I write and say, but in the last three years— the length of time I've been critical of the bungled process of unification and warned of its mindless speed—I've been forced to realize that I've been writing and speaking in a vacuum. My own loyalty, not to the state but to its constitution, was unwanted.

I freely admit that this sense of talking in a vacuum is a new experience for me, and not one I particularly enjoy. Was it ever different? Yes! For a few years, when Willy Brandt was Chancellor, and tried to put the programme of his government—'Dare to be more democratic!'—into effect. For Willy Brandt, contact with intellectuals was an essential stimulant: when still Mayor of Berlin, he and his wife Ruth hosted discussions that were critical and frank and shattered a few Berliner illusions. 'Political culture' is a hollow phrase nowadays, but for a time then it meant something and we listened to one another—another one of Willy Brandt's virtues.

When the writer Siegfried Lenz and I accompanied him as Chancellor to Warsaw in 1970, we felt we had more than an ornamental function: because Lenz and I had both accepted the loss of our homeland, we brought with us recognition of Poland's western borders. Were we proud of Germany then? Yes, looking back I'm proud to have been with that party in Warsaw. But as I try to remember that brief, important time, I realize I'm talking about a lost era. With his death, Willy Brandt made the loss still clearer to me.

More losses: what happened to diversity of opinion? Nowadays the editorial lines of the papers are indistinguishable; they save their trivial disagreements for coy sub-clauses. The huffy dismissal of the democratic left is part of the *bon ton* today. One Fatherland, one *feuilleton*.

Also in the list of losses I would cite the Bundestag's decision to transfer the capital from Bonn to Berlin, and the tacit overturning of this decision by current Bonn practice. It is a circus in which the President of the Bundestag is the ringmaster, and the media are performers. The expensive hall for future debates has been inaugurated. But everything else goes on as before. Meanwhile, east of the Elbe, the child has fallen into the well.

The child has fallen into the well, and it is screaming. What is it screaming? It is screaming for *more*. People here in the west avert their ears. Have we Germans become so alienated from one another that all we care about are our own petty interests and possessions? And could it be that the coolness between Germans has produced the current, disgraceful xenophobia directed against those other strangers whom we call foreigners?

I walked off my rage about Rostock on the Danish holiday island; later I tried to etch it into copper plates with a cold needle: scratching as therapy.

But when my rage cooled, sadness and anger still remained. And accordingly, my notes demanded: What have you done to my country? How did this failed union come about? What madness prompted the electorate to entrust this difficult and politically demanding task to a fat figure-masseur? What slick director turned our disunited land into a subject for chat shows? What dull-wittedness got us to pile the injustices of our capitalist system on top of those of 'real socialism'? What's the matter with us?

Perhaps we lack the very people we're afraid of, because they are foreign to us and look foreign. Those whom, out of fear, we meet with hatred, which now daily turns to violence. And perhaps those we most lack are the ones we think of as the lowest of the low, the Romanies and the Sinti, the gypsies.

They have no allies. No politician represents their case, whether in the European Parliament or the Bundestag. No state they can appeal to would support their demands for compensation—pathetic, isn't it?—for Auschwitz, or make them a national priority.

The Romanies and Sinti are the lowest of the low. 'Expel them!' says Herr Seiters and gets on the line to Romania. 'Smoke them out!' shout the skinheads. But in Romania and everywhere else, gypsies are bottom of the heap as well. Why?

Because they are different. Because they steal, are restless, roam, have the Evil Eye and that stunning beauty that makes us ugly to ourselves. Because their mere existence puts our values into question. Because they are all very well in operas and operettas, but in reality—it sounds awful, reminds you of awfulness—they are antisocial, odd and don't fit in. 'Torch them!' shout the skinheads.

When Heinrich Böll was laid to rest seven years ago, there was a gypsy band leading the pall-bearers—Lev Kopelev, Günter Wallraff, myself and Böll's sons, and the mourners on the way to the graveyard. It was Böll's wish. It was what he wanted to play

Opposite: Warsaw, December 1970. Willy Brandt pays tribute to the Jewish insurgents killed by the Nazis during the ghetto uprising in 1943.

him into the grave, that deeply tragic, despairingly gay music. It has taken me until now to understand him.

Let half a million and more Sinti and Romanies live among us. We need them. They could help us by irritating our rigid order a little. Something of their way of life could rub off on us. They could teach us how meaningless frontiers are: careless of boundaries, Romanies and Sinti are at home all over Europe. They are what we claim to be: born Europeans!

Translated from the German by Michael Hofmann

ED KASHI
BERLIN BY NIGHT

GRANTA

MONIKA MARON
ZONOPHOBIA

Since I've been able to travel from East to West, I've begun to take an interest in who it was who wanted Germany split and why: why the Left, the French, the Russians, the English, the unifiers of Western Europe wanted it; everyone in fact, apart from, presumably, most of the people in East Germany.

Of course, unification has become a nightmare, although not because its opponents were right: not the Left or the French, the English or Russians; and not because the chemical-workers of Saxony can no longer spend their time tinkering with dripping acid-pipes and are out of work; and not because rents are rising, speculators are enjoying a boom and mediocre academics from Western Wherever are occupying East German teaching posts: that's all to be expected.

Unification has become a nightmare for me because the East, wherever it articulates itself in those terms, gives me an inescapable feeling of nausea. Everything has turned into nausea: my pity, my sympathy, my interest. I know I'm being unfair and I can't do anything about it. I see it as a sickness and don't know the cure. I call the sickness—an allergy to the eastern zone—zonophobia.

I'm going to try to describe my symptoms honestly. Someone else can work out whether the defect lies in the observer or the observed or both. I'm going to assume the right to unfairness.

Stubborn defiance and pedantic zeal are the current trademarks of behaviour in the East. I know my countrymen on the *autobahn* from Hamburg to Berlin, without having to decipher their number-plates: anyone driving along unflustered in the left-hand lane is from the East. What you have, you own—even if it's the left-hand lane. Anyone making a death-defying left turn at a junction, with no concern for the herds of BMWs and Porches charging towards him, is from the East. He's showing how much he understands.

If my masochistic curiosity takes me shopping in the supermarket in Pankow—formerly state-run, now Spar—and I watch them, securing their provisions, I have to stop myself from

Opposite: Berlin, 14 November 1989. East Berliners cross over to the West.

Photo: Leonard Freed (Magnum)

grabbing out of their baskets the nauseatingly big packs of meat and the sweet sparkling Balkan plonk. I'd like to ask the sulky woman, who's just run over my toes with her trolley and then given me a dirty look, why she hasn't apologized. Or the man I nearly collided with: 'Why don't you smile?' I walk among them like an anxious hostess—smile and apologize, apologize and smile—hoping they will one day understand my message.

It's even worse when hunger forces me into the torture-chambers of East German gastronomy. If the food is remotely edible, a reference to the class of the establishment appears on the menu—class as in the second syllable of the phrase 'world-class'. So anyone who wanders into, say, the new restaurant in the former council of state building in Niedershonhausen—where they won't allow us to sit five to a table not quite large enough to accommodate us, because we then spoil the ambience—knows it has class. Friends of mine who aren't genuine Easterners often say I'm exaggerating or I should be more understanding. I, on the other hand, think my friends' forbearance is naïve. They have no idea what a miserable life you lead under the dictatorship of waiters, bus-conductors and taxi-drivers. It may sound frivolous but I suffered less under the Stasi than I have under our new united-German waiters, bus-conductors and taxi-drivers. I could ignore the Stasi; I didn't know them.

You see, my former fellow-citizens believe that the rest of the world owes them something, most particularly their dignity. They have forgotten that until three years ago they were perfectly prepared to treat their dignity in a pretty cavalier fashion, which is how they lost it in the first place. Now they think Helmut Kohl has found it but won't give it back.

When they say 'dignity', though, they probably mean something else: it's their familiar equality that they're really missing. When they all had less rather than more, but all the same amount, then they all felt they were of equal value. One of the most common statements in this country used to be: 'You think you're something special.' No one was special; everyone was as clever as everyone else. In matters of taste and culture the claim that we lived in a proletarian dictatorship was true. Suddenly that's all over, and it's a hard thing to bear.

For as long as I lived among them, my fellow East Germans hid this extraordinary sensitivity to issues of social injustice. They buried it under their dullness and tolerance, their moral cowardice and their pusillanimous sense of order. I should be pleased now that they're calling an injustice an injustice and a lie a lie. But when I see their fury, spluttering in their Saxon dialect on the television, saying that no one, but no one, can hoodwink or exploit them—all this expressed with characteristic East German manly verve, to prove to all those effete West German strangers out there who is now calling the shots—then I can't help thinking of them slinking off to the ballot-boxes, sitting with downcast eyes in their meetings, hoodwinked, exploited, humiliated. Once, it would never have occurred to them to go on strike.

For every misfortune an enemy is created to blame. For want of imagination they've chosen the one that was drummed into them for decades: the West. The West isn't paying enough, the West is sending us the wrong people, the West is flogging our assets. They only have to look eastwards to know how bad things could get. But just as they're unconcerned that people are dying in the Balkans, that Russians are starving, that Hungarians, Poles, Czechs and Slovaks have hard times ahead of them, so are they equally unaware that the salesgirls in Hamburg are striking for near-subsistence wages, that the higher salaries in the West are swallowed up by the even higher rents, that the extra taxes that were added for their benefit are a huge sacrifice to people who aren't doing one bit better than they are themselves, even if they live in Cologne or Bochum and are given the nickname 'Wessis'—a synonym for rich.

'Kohl promised'—that's the most embarrassing, shameful, ridiculous phrase of the last two years. Every opposition politician who uses it against Helmut Kohl should be aware that he is turning the East Germans into silly, disappointed children, whinging because they've been given the wrong Christmas present. Helmut Kohl made a promise that he hasn't kept. So what? Who forced them to believe Kohl? What reason did they have, after forty years of the GDR, to believe any politician more than they believed their own eyes? They knew their factories,

cities and houses best; they themselves should have told Kohl he
was wrong or lying when he claimed the GDR would turn into the
Garden of Eden within three or four years, without a hike in taxes.
And what decisions would they have made instead if they hadn't
believed him? Would they have wanted to abandon monetary
union and unification and the hundreds of billions flowing into
this little country while the giant Russian empire has to beg to
have the payment on the interest on their hundred-billion loan
deferred?

Sometimes I think the opponents of unification were right:
the East Germans should have been left to go through all the
miseries that had to follow the collapse of communism on their
own, so that they could finally learn that their own action and
inaction have consequences, as did their earlier passivity and
silence. Instead they have simply mistaken the new authorities for
the old ones. They chose this government. If they belatedly come
to see it as an error of judgement, they, like everyone else, should
learn how to correct it: at the next election.

Having expressed my unfair fury, I feel a need for balance. I
met a young man recently in my old street in Pankow. He
looked familiar to me, and, as I was wondering which of
my son's friends he could be, he said, 'Don't you recognize me?
I'm the postman.' He seemed to know he was hardly recognizable.

Four or five years ago, when he was still our postman, I knew
him as a pale, shy boy in a velvet-collared coat that was too small
for him, weighed down by his postbag and a seriousness ill-suited
to his youth. Once he rang the doorbell and asked if I could lend
him a book of mine. Later I met him at one of my readings in a
church.

If I failed to recognize him, it wasn't his new clothes, his
different hairstyle or his round sun-glasses. He walked differently,
talked differently; he was different.

I asked him what he was up to these days.

He was studying classical philology, he said. It had long been
a dream of his.

I don't know if the quiet triumph I thought I heard was in his
voice or if I added it myself. He was one of those who had wasted

Photo: Popperfoto

away in the old East because they had refused military service or kept out of the German Youth Federation; who were, at worst, shot trying to get over the Wall and who, at best, wrote poems about unfulfilled dreams. Now he looked back at the scene of his involuntary life as a postman, as the person he had always wanted to be. He was glad, he said. He was just glad. And I was glad too, glad that my postman is fulfilling his vocation, glad that we have unification.

Translated from the German by Shaun Whiteside

GRANTA

HANS JOACHIM ELLERBROCK
HALLE BY DAY

Halle is the fourth largest city in the former East Germany, with a population of 340,000. Many of these people, perhaps one third, live in pre-fabricated houses, designed to last only twenty-five years. These neighbourhoods were constructed to accommodate the labour force of the chemical giants BUNA and LEUNA which are based in Halle. Partly as a result of emissions from these plants, but more particularly because brown coal is burnt in private houses, Halle has the highest level of air pollution in Germany. Since unification 15,000 chemical workers have lost their jobs; more redundancies are expected. In Halle's shops everything is now available.

GRANTA

MAX THOMAS MEHR
AND REGINE SYLVESTER
THE STONE-THROWER FROM
EISENHUTTENSTADT

Last year, a photograph was published on the back page of a Berlin daily. It depicted a German mother from the town of Eisenhuttenstadt—strongly built and dressed in loose jogging clothes—grabbing hold of her skinhead son and dragging him away from the hostel for asylum-seekers that he and his friends had been attacking with rocks.

Another picture of the same boy appeared a little later. In fact, the boy kept popping up in the press—sometimes with a kerchief wrapped over his face, sometimes without—in *Stern, Die Tagezeitung*, on television. But it was that first photograph that everyone remembered: mothers do not drive to the front lines to drag away their children by the scruff of the neck. Journalists Max Thomas Mehr and Regine Sylvester spent two days in Eisenhuttenstadt looking for the famous mother of the skinhead son and persuaded her—along with her husband and son—to talk to them. They met in a restaurant with loud music and a single grumpy waitress and began by asking the mother what she was telling her son as the picture was taken.

Mother: I was telling him that enough was enough and that it was now time to go home. The car was waiting and his mates would never know that he'd left. But then he bent down to pick up a stone and that's when I grabbed him. As I was pulling him away, a photographer suddenly appeared out of nowhere.

Son: I took care of him.

Mother: I drove him home but the moment we got there he went straight back.

Son: It had finished by then.

Mother: Thank God, the photograph wasn't published in the local paper.

Interviewers: Why?

Mother: Because a lot of people know us here.

Interviewers: But you tried to make your son stop. You did a good thing. Not many people would have done that.

135

Mother: I want to know what the boy was doing there in the first place! Don't think he was there with my permission. My husband and I had been waiting for him to come home—for hours. Finally, my husband went to bed. It was one in the morning and still our son hadn't returned. That was when I got the car and went out looking for him. My husband never knew I went out. His workmates told him the next day. He was ashamed.

Father: They showed the two of them on Breakfast Television and later on the news as well.

Interviewers: Why did you feel ashamed?

Mother: Because your friends then think you can't control your own son.

Father: Something like that.

Mother: It has nothing to do with the question of the foreigners. No one in Eisenhuttenstadt wants the foreigners here.

Interviewers: What do you do?

Father: I'm a driver for EKO [*Eisenhuttenstadt Kombinat Ost*]. I've been doing it for twenty years. Shift-work.

Mother: I'm at EKO, too, at least until June. We're demolishing the fourth blast furnace. I process the payslips.

Interviewers: Did you speak to anyone at work about the incident?

Mother: No. There was an article about it, but no one realized that it referred to me, even though everyone was talking about it. One of the women I work with said that she would have done the same thing.

Interviewers: Did you have many disagreements with your son?

Mother: This isn't the first time.

Interviewers: What do you know about the people in the hostel?

Son: I see them on TV, wearing shawls and rubbishy clothes.

Interviewers: How did the trouble ever begin in the first place?

Son: The trouble started with the hostel itself. It's so overcrowded. But we didn't throw stones in the beginning. No one threw stones until after Rostock.

Interviewers: Don't you think it's wrong to throw stones at children?

Son: They weren't the target. We were throwing stones at the Border Police. If there were no Border Police, there would be no trouble. It's the Border Police who protect the hostels. Without them, the hostels would be empty. Everyone would have run off by now.

Interviewers: To where?

Son: I don't know. The hills.

Interviewers: What hills? Why are you so vicious?

Mother: He's not vicious. He has good feelings too. It's just that he has to say things like this. It's the fashion, the way people think today. Look at him yourself. What would you do if you were him?

   We have a good relationship—except that he runs away. He's only fifteen. He started running away two years ago.

Interviewers: And then you lost him?

Mother: It was when the Wall came down. That's when he got attracted to the Right.

Interviewers: Were there foreigners in Eisenhuttenstadt before the Wall came down?

Son: Vietnamese and Algerians. A few Vietnamese are still here.

Interviewers: Did your family have any contact with foreigners?

Mother: No.

Son: Aunt Doris's husband.

Mother: Well, him.

Interviewers: Where does Aunt Doris's husband come from?

Mother: He's a Yugoslav. I've got nothing against foreigners. I've worked with them.

Interviewers: But never socialized?

Mother: A friend of mine had a Moroccan boyfriend and I went out with them once or twice. We've got nothing against foreigners. They can come and work here and then go home, and that's fine. Or they come here to learn something they can't do at home. That's what the Vietnamese did. But they shouldn't stay here.

Son: Do you realize that that hostel is supposed to hold seven hundred and they've got two thousand two hundred of them in there?

Mother: You see whole gangs of foreign women using the dustbins. They pull up their skirts and do their business there.

Son: There are garden allotments at the back. More than a hundred have been broken into since foreigners started arriving.

Mother: And it's not just here. I used to accompany groups of children to holiday camps in Poland. I took my own children too. When we arrived there they would shout: 'Nazis go home!'

Father: The same thing happened in Czechoslovakia and Hungary.

Mother: You can't go on blaming us for what happened. I wasn't alive then.

Father: It's history.

Mother: They should let bygones be bygones. Can't they let us forget that we lost the war?

Son: At least the children of *Gastarbeiter* should push off home. There are gangs of them in West Berlin, Black Panthers and stuff.

Interviewers: Those children were born here. They don't think of themselves as foreigners.

Mother: How many foreigners live here now?

Interviewers: Barely one per cent. In some cities like Frankfurt am

Photo: Hans-Georg Gaul

138

Main it's twenty-five per cent.

Mother: Well, we're the ones who are treated like dirt now. Today I read in the paper that they'll probably be closing the iron works here. That'll be curtains for the whole town.

Son: I think they should take those two thousand two hundred foreigners and ship them to Bonn. Let's see how they like it.

Interviewers: Do you actually live near the asylum hostel?

Mother: No, it's quite a long way away.

Son: It's not that far. We may not actually live next to the hostel, but we see people from it every day in town. Day before yesterday I saw another one sniffing round in the rubbish.

Interviewers: Were you happy when the Wall came down?

Son: Yes, it meant I could go to see the West.

Mother: I'd always seen the West on TV. I wanted to see the original.

Son: I went to Krenzberg, but there were hardly any German shops. I wanted to buy a cassette but they only had ones with Turkish writing on them. And at the Alexanderplatz today all you see is Yugoslav beggars and con artists.

Interviewers: Why do you always see them and not the Italian pizza parlours and Greek restaurants?

Son: Don't want to see them, do I? When the GDR existed you could get a bratwurst at any kiosk. Today, it's almost impossible.

Interviewers: Is your parents' life different now that the Wall has come down?

Son: They were moaning before and now they're moaning again. How can they stand it, being lied to and cheated all the time by the politicians and the fat cats.

Interviewers: Who do you trust?

Son: My mates.

Interviewers: What would make life better for you and your parents?

Son: They would have to bring in some fairer law about asylum seekers. Even if people really are persecuted, they still can't let in as many as they're letting in now. If someone comes from some country where there's no political persecution he shouldn't even be allowed into Germany. They should rebuild industry and not spend years talking about it. Stop handing out credits to countries who only waste them anyway. Yeah, what else would I do? The German territories in the east should be returned.

Interviewers: Why?

Son: There's a housing shortage.

Interviewers: But there are people living in those places now.

Son: If they're Poles, they should go back to Poland. If they're Germans, they can stay. The Poles have settled on our patch.

Interviewers: I saw a pained expression on your face as your son spoke.

Father: They're not my views.

Interviewers: He's your son.

Father: I wonder where he gets them from.

Son: Once Germany's re-established we can develop the eastern territories. Then we'd be a bigger country.

Interviewers: Why do you want Germany to be so big?

Son: Israelis are saying stuff about Germany again.

Interviewers: Why do you want Germany to be big?

Son: You tell me why Germany should be small then.

Interviewers: It isn't small. Lots of countries are smaller.

Son: The Germans are always too quick to cave in. I don't get it. They should be proud of themselves. Look at German history. No other country has done anything like that.

Mother: Where do you get all this from?

Son: Books.

Interviewers: What's an average day like for you?

Son: Right now, when I'm not working, I stay in bed till eleven or twelve. Then I go over to my mate's. We chat, have a beer, mooch around.

Interviewers: And in the afternoon?

Son: We meet up again.

Interviewers: And in the evening?

Son: Well, we stick around together.

Interviewers: Doing what?

Son: We talk. Sit in the garage, listen to records. Sometimes we drive over to Guben and go down the disco.

Interviewers: If you meet up with Poles is there a fight?

Son: The Poles don't show their face there.

Interviewers: What's changed for you since '89?

Son: Loads of things. I can do more stuff.

Interviewers: But you just told us you never do anything.

Son: Sometimes we can't think of anything to do.

Interviewers: Can you imagine how you'd like to live when you're your parents' age?

Son: How d'you mean?

Interviewers: Family?

Son: Sure. Car, job, kids.

Interviewers: A wife?

Son: A German wife.

Translated from the German by Michael Hofmann

HAS MY CHILD BECOME A NEO-NAZI?
A Checklist for Parents

Looks: Your child gets a very short hair-cut. He goes around in a green or black bomber jacket, instead of the usual denim one. He may ask you to sew badges on it (an Iron Cross, for instance). He stops wearing trainers; he wants Doc Martens with steel toecaps and white laces. Suddenly, he's into white T-shirts with German slogans. OUR TIP: Don't deny him anything (or he'll want it even more).

Music: Records by *Storkraft* [Disruptive Force] and *Noie Werte* [New Values] appear in his collection. You'll be able to spot them: they'll have skulls and swastikas on their covers. One day you hear your child sing: 'One day the world will see/Adolf Hitler was right'. His new catchphrase is 'Oi! Oi!'. OUR TIP: Listen! Talk about the lyrics with him.

Opinions: When shots of refugees appear on the television news, your child suddenly looks interested. He asks, 'What do they want here, anyway?' OUR TIP: Watch what you say, and don't tell anti-foreigner jokes.

Room: Your child takes down his pop posters and puts up ones of World War II instead. He sends away for the Reich's wartime flag. Baseball bats appear in a corner of his room (no baseballs, though). Instead of *Bravo*, there are fanzines on his bedside table: *Kraft durch Froide* ('Strength through Joy'), *Frontal, Der Kampftrinker* ('The Battle-Drinker'), *Yah—Skin Reports.* OUR TIP: don't take the fanzines away. Ask him to describe the more interesting feature stories.

Habits: Your child is out late every night, and always in his favourite gear. He talks about 'new friends' and develops a sudden interest in the martial arts. OUR TIP: give him a treat. Buy him a membership in a sports club (karate's OK) or a computer game. Have his 'new friends' over for dinner.

Reprinted from *Bild*, 3 December, the day after Lars Christiansen, nineteen, was arrested for the murder of three Turkish women in Mölln.

Is Britain Rotting from the Inside?

In a word - YES. The way the government shut the mines, defended the pound, while claiming a mandate with 42 per cent of the vote, is intolerable.

Now the Matrix Churchill affair has revealed how deep the rot has gone.

Ministers and civil servants believe that they can get away with it - that they can change policy in secret, jail the innocent, deceive the public, and then bully MPs into voting for them should they be exposed.

Michael Heseltine's claim that all governments behave like this is a damning indictment of our system. Power corrupts, absolute power corrupts absolutely, and the absolute sovereignty of the House of Commons has corrupted the British regime. It must be changed.

We must wake this country from its torpor. There is a proud tradition of freedom and liberty, of democracy and fairness, in Britain. But it can be restored only by a democratic written constitution.

Help us make it happen. Together we can stop the rot. Add your name to

CHARTER 88

Charter 88 is a citizens' movement for a democratic written constitution. Our demands include a call for a Bill of Rights, electoral reform and accountable and devolved power. If you want to join us, use the leaflet in this issue or write to: *Charter 88, Exmouth House, 3 Pine Street, London, EC1R 0JH*

KLAUS SCHLESINGER
A HIPPY AMONG COMMUNISTS

In March 1975, thirty years after the collapse of German fascism, N., a student from Berlin—bearded and long-haired—attended a series of lectures at a university on the Baltic coast. He missed his return train and was forced to make a stop in A., a town on the border of what used to be Pomerania. During the war A. had been three-quarters destroyed. Most of its inhabitants were refugees from areas occupied by the German Reich.

The student had two hours to wait for his connection. He wandered into the station-bar to get some lunch. There were only a few people in the bar, all of them locals, and the moment the student walked in every one of them fell silent. Then, from a corner of the room, the quiet was broken with an insult. Other remarks followed. Each of the comments addressed the student's appearance and each was voiced loudly, without the slightest inhibition. The student ignored the comments and sat down to read his newspaper. A drunk approached his table and enquired about the student's washing habits. Another man shouted across that were the student a woman he would refuse intimacy with him. N. asked if he might be allowed to eat his lunch in peace. Everyone present roared with laughter. The drunk leaned closer and reached out to pull at the student's beard, to see if it was real. The student jumped up and ran from the room.

The square in front of the station was quiet and empty. The student decided to walk into the town. Two men painting an iron railing dismissed him with a shake of the head. Children playing football in a field interrupted their game to point at him. When he stopped at a kiosk to change money for the telephone the girl refused to help or even speak to him.

It was Saturday and the high street shops were crowded. To avoid stares the student found himself looking into shop windows. The window of the photographer's shop made him pause. There were a number of wedding photographs on display and the student was surprised how images from his grandmother's photograph album—pictures he hadn't seen for years—came into his mind.

Half an hour before his train was due to leave the student

returned to the station. He was angry at how he had been greeted in the town but wondered if he had exaggerated the hatred he had felt; perhaps he was still shaken from his experience in the bar.

In the square there was an elderly man. The man had his back to the student but hearing his footsteps he turned round to face him. He was powerfully built, perhaps in his late sixties. His eyes were deep-set and reddened by drink. As the student approached the old man looked bewildered, even astonished. He slapped his hand to his head as if to awaken some long-submerged memory, something that would help him identify this extraordinary phenomenon. Suddenly, as if inspired, he stepped forward and stood in front of the student, blocking his path to the station. Speaking quietly he then asked the student whether.he was a Jew

The student ignored the question and tried to brush past the old man. The old man repeated his question, more vociferously this time. The student quickened his pace but the old man followed him, running, all the way into the station, all the time repeating a single word, shouting it: 'Jew!'

Translated from the German by Shaun Whiteside

WOLF BIERMANN
SHAKING HANDS WITH
THE ZEITGEIST

Down here on the Elbe, not far from the jetties, with a view across the river towards the famous old shipyard of Blohm & Voss, looms a monster of modern architecture, a floating dock on dry land, cloaked expensively in stainless-steel plate. This is the new headquarters of publishers Gruner & Jahr. In this shipyard it's news they pop-rivet together; stories are welded, sensations launched. The chimney belches smoke. There's no recession here. This is a place where fairytales come true: it's the headquarters of *Stern* magazine. Every week millions hand over their small change for a helping of the brightly coloured sweet-and-sour stew, concocted from the spittle of the murderer, from mothers' tears, from the broth of catastrophe, the sweat of the holiday-maker, the blood of the asylum-seeker and enriched with the flesh of accident victims. It is a piquant stew, which may be thinned according to taste with canned extract of international tits and bums.

It was to this temple of the media that my wife Pamela and I had been invited for a reception in honour of the Czar-without-a-Country. Where the Hamburg City Council had tried and failed, Bertelsmann, Germany's mightiest media concern, had succeeded: Mikhail Sergejevitch Gorbachev himself in the Free and Hanseatic City of Hamburg! No doubt the media gods had lured him there with a cheque to endow some perestroika foundation in Moscow, on whose behalf the unemployed ex-President is now moonlighting.

This was the first invitation of its kind I had ever received. To tell the truth, I hadn't the slightest intention of going. But my wife saw through my foolish arrogance and defended the basic human right to indulge in a little vanity and the occasional piece of hype. What was more, it might be the only chance we would ever get to meet a *Homo Historicus* of Gorbachev's calibre. He was, after all, more than a mere hiccup in the history of the world.

I gave in. I trimmed my beard and presented myself at the appointed time and place. Looking back now, I am shocked at how authentic my version of events has become, how easily and deceitfully memory transforms an awkward encounter into a skilled and accomplished performance. The boasts to an audience of credulous grandchildren are effortlessly created: 'Ah yes, when I met the great Gorbachev himself I held out my hand and said, "Put it there, old son!" Shy? Not a bit! But Christ, old Gorby had a handshake like a tractor driver from the Red Dawn collective farm.'

Photo: Popperfoto

And over the years the episode is embellished and exaggerated until in the end the fibber comes to believe it himself. Who hasn't experienced this? The initial impression made by a meeting with an extraordinary person is deep enough, but the imagination immediately sets to work retouching the memory. The incident puffs itself up into a miniature myth. The hero's fleeting smile has, twenty years on, broadened into a deep friendship; the passing of time turns a disparaging glance into a bitter feud. And a hasty handshake assumes the significance of a turning point in world history.

Was it in 1803? It must have been around then that poor Friedrich Hölderlin set out on foot for Bordeaux to take up the post of private tutor to the family of the Bremen consul. Hölderlin was halfway through his life and already teetering on the edge of madness. In any case, our poet did not take the usual route, via Paris, but chose to go the long way round, passing through Lyons. Why? Jean-Pierre Lefebvre, an authority on Hölderlin, may have found the answer.

In those very days none other than Napoleon Bonaparte was staying in Lyons on state business. Lefebvre's thesis is this: perhaps our roving, sentimental, liberty-loving poet was seized by the desire to see the true liberator of the age, or even to breathe the same city air. But poor Hölderlin missed Napoleon (styled by his friend Hegel as the 'Zeitgeist on Horseback'), if only narrowly, by two or three days.

Yours truly is neither so hard-up for money nor as richly talented. I haven't quite yet lost faith in this crazy world and I've never had to walk for weeks on end across it. If we were going to gawp at Gorbachev, the Zeitgeist on his Knees, then we would go in style. For twelve marks eighty we took a taxi from Altona, where we live, to the Baumwall down in the docks area. World history comes cheap in Hamburg.

The distinguished guest was given the red-carpet treatment. The chairman of the board of directors, a Mr Gerd Schulte-Hillen, and his newspaper men, enjoyed with Anglo-Saxon reserve the scalp they had shipped in. The sight of the genuine Gorbachev clearly gave them visible relief; it was not so long since they'd published Hitler's diaries. Something like a hundred VIPs and spouses had been invited. The police cordons were almost on the East Berlin scale of old.

Gorbachev's speech was the centre-piece of the evening. He spoke partly without notes, in the calm voice of a man who is used to being listened to. It was a speech without sparkle or depth. I stared at the dark red birth mark on his shiny bald head and thought how much it really did look like the map of something which the Japanese or the Azeris or Ukrainians

153

wanted to tear from the Union.

Gorby gave a variation on his popular metaphor of the European House. He explained to the assembled opinion-makers that the European House had many rooms. Staying with the anaemic image, he appealed to the generosity of the wealthy Germans who lived on the first floor. I think the Hanseatic VIPs and their wives were a little disappointed; his speech was like a Baltic beach at the end of the season: lots of sand, every kind of empty plastic bottle, a sprinkling of sweet-wrappers—but not a single precious stone. It demonstrated that quality of the hero in world history that our philosopher Hegel noted: they never know what they are doing. (If they did know, they probably wouldn't do it.) In his time, of course, Gorbachev gave the world two galvanizing catchwords: glasnost and perestroika. He also provided two rousing sentences: 'We need democracy, like the air, to breathe'—that was one. And the second, about Honecker & Co: 'Life punishes whoever comes too late.' The tritest commonplaces, launched into the world at the right historical moment, become magic spells.

But on this occasion Gorbachev bequeathed nothing to the treasury of quotations. He spoke about the role of the Russians in the shattered Soviet Union. He explained how Russia's rebirth was essential to the future of its neighbouring countries, if not the whole world. It may be that I am over-sensitive, but when I heard that, I thought: hopefully the Russian Jews will survive such a renaissance as well. I had the chance to put that question to him, rhetorically, in the little speech with which I introduced Eva-Maria Hagen, who performed a droll song for Gorbachev and his wife, one I wrote four years ago, which begins with the words, '*Mikhail Gorbachev, are you fish or are you fowl?*' So that he could understand some of it, we shoved a rough Russian translation into his hand.

Dinner was then served: a simple banquet with anchovy *vol-au-vents* and smoked salmon and hand-shelled shrimps.

Finally, over pudding, I had convinced myself: the intellectual barrenness of Gorby's speech did no harm at all. On the

Photo: Associated Press Photos

contrary, it was rather cheering. Everyone could now see that even a true saviour of the world was only an ordinary human being. It proved that almost any alert mind can star in history if only Mr Chance, the director, casts him. Mikhail Gorbachev performed his big role long ago. On this particular evening he might just as well have philosophized to the assembled fish heads about Hamburg eel soup or Russian buckwheat porridge; his place in the pantheon of humanity is secure.

And, of course, he deserves our respect, because he brought the genocidal East–West conflict to an end. He cleared the path to disarmament and he deprived the omnipotent Communist Party of power. Even if he was only half-aware of what he was doing. His inconsistency towards the Stalinist hardliners was also

155

no bad thing. By expressions of loyalty to the Party, by his scandalous tactics in the Baltic states, by boxing Yeltsin's ears, he confused the military. He let them hope that the good old bad old days would return. Conversely, by endlessly hob-nobbing with the hardliners he prevented political reforms and annoyed the intellectual élite. His suicidal tolerance finally encouraged the old guard to carry out the coup. But by the time his intimate enemies dared attempt regicide, it was already too late. The old gang lost everything.

Despite all his weaknesses, mistakes and possible crimes, Gorbachev is a dragon killer. He was also, of course, once a Stalinist *apparatchik*. In such a system no one got to the top without guilt or crime. (The liberal Shevardnadze was once a feared KGB boss in Georgia.) But let the Balts and the Georgians and all the Russians spit on their liberator—I admire him. We Germans owe him everything. Without the radical transformation of Big Brother all the Johnny-come-lately literary heroes in East Berlin would probably only have turned into freedom fighters in their graves.

The party for Gorbachev dribbled on for a while. Eventually the opportunity arose for some small talk. Here at last was my chance to clarify everything. To my astonishment, someone introduced me as 'the German Vyssotski'. My name seemed to trigger a memory—perhaps the scandal of my expulsion from the GDR more than fifteen years ago—and I was excited and happy and solemn. My heart beat in my skull, my brain was overwhelmed by a tidal wave of emotions. In such circumstances words of conversation are, anyway, only crude identification marks amid the headlong rush of protocol. How are people supposed to talk to one another, if they don't even have the time to be silent together? Which is all to say: I embarrassed myself. I said to this complete stranger a sentence which I had believed could never pass my lips again. My four words were spoken as a kind of reflex action, like a dying soldier giving a password; the thirteen letters fell from my mouth like teeth that had been knocked out. Before me stood the last torchbearer of Communist ideology. I said: 'I am a Communist.'

Photo: Popperfoto

Years of despair and hope culminated in that moment: Gorbachev embodied all the wild thoughts and shouting matches of three decades. A film was running inside my head, beginning with my first doubts after the Twentieth Congress of the Communist Party of the Soviet Union in 1956 and ending with the crushing certainty that the Communist heaven on earth could be nothing but perfect hell.

But as failed Communists is our place in world history therefore as contemptible as that of our old great enemies the Nazis? Of course not! We were always better and also always worse. Put more precisely: our crimes were all the worse, because they stemmed from a better tradition. The Nazis grew out of the blood-stained stupidity of racial delusion, and they remained true to their colours. Hitler honestly promised the extermination of the Jews and held to it. When the war was already lost, when he

157

needed every truck and every locomotive to supply the Wehrmacht, he still requisitioned enough trains to transport the Jews to the death camps. If that was not devotion to principles!

We, however, betrayed everything that we ever promised. We emerged from the humane tradition of the Enlightenment. Our intellectual fathers were the radical democrats of the French Revolution, our poets Heine and Büchner, our thinkers Karl Marx and Rosa Luxemburg. Communism and Social Democracy were siblings in the same historical family: but the intolerant son became a much-admired murderer and the prim sister an unloved wallflower.

It causes me the deepest sadness and is to our everlasting shame that no one liquidated so many Communists as the Communists. Hitler murdered a total of 64,000 German Communists. But Stalin's executioners murdered almost the whole of Lenin's Central Committee and liquidated a couple of million cadres as well. The Nazis did not butcher their own people, apart from a few individual cases. And what was butchered in the Communist workers' movement was a fundamental humane tendency, which historically never existed in Fascism.

We failed. Now any kind of hope for a more just society seems to be discredited until the end of the world. Despite all that, this ruined childish hope is still close to my heart. The best and bravest and cleverest people who created me were almost all left-wing rebels and undogmatic spirits, all of them burnt children of Communism. And when I met the last representative of the Communist Party of the Soviet Union, the old wounds burst open again and bled. And it was far from melodramatic, on the contrary; it was a confusingly pleasant pain.

'I am a Communist.' And see: Gorbachev responded to the stimulus like a Pavlovian dog in the Party academy. The little red bell struck, and the old ideological saliva flowed. It seemed to me as if a romantic revolutionary spasm passed through his body. He had evidently not been expecting this signal from his past here in Hamburg. Suddenly he gained a firmer grip on my hand and, looking through my eyes deep into my heart as if through reversed opera glasses, he squeezed meaningfully and tragically, communicating what we both knew very well: it doesn't matter any more.

Photo: Popperfoto

Am I exaggerating? No, Gorbachev's handshake was really something! It was a worker's handshake. No, wrong! Real workers shake hands without the noble proletarian emphasis, which Gorbachev had.

One often hears the claim that at the very last moment of life, all of the past rushes through the dying person's head once again as a compressed, abbreviated film. I did not at all feel like dying, but I did see a speeded-up film as Gorbachev gripped my hand in a vice: a film of the death of the Communist idea. Our handshake lasted at most three seconds—but for me it became an epic to fill a whole evening.

It was a remarkable handshake; it bore a resemblance to the ones I knew from officials of the labour movement, who shake hands to show that inside they are still workers. Intellectuals who had picked up important posts in the Party or the trade unions exaggerated the proletarian manner, disguising their genteel mitts by gripping all the more resolutely. They took the hand of the unsuspecting so skilfully, that with a relatively small expenditure of energy they could still crush the victim's fingers. This hyperproletarian trick worked especially well on women. The loyal party handshake also had a formative effect on the arts. Party artists painted monumental workers' hands, with which no real worker could compete. State actors, playing class conscious workers in Socialist Realist films, shook hands with this gusto.

Photo: Associated Press Photos

The true Noble Proletarian Handshake begins long before the actual pressing of flesh. It is clearly developing as the proletarian handshaker approaches the person to be greeted. The proferred arm displays two indispensable components: it must be extended somewhat further than normal, and the elbow must point outwards and upwards a little. This signals the strength of the working class hidden beneath the jacket, the mighty arm and shoulder muscles of the steelworker or miner. At the same time it's noticeable that the fingers are unusually far apart. This gesture has its origin in the fact that the reliable comrade worker is distinguished by the noble mark of primitive manual labour: his massive hands. These calloused digits have only a moment

GRANTA

Every issue of Granta features fiction, politics, travel writing, photography and more. So don't miss out — subscribe today and save up to 40% from the £7.99 cover price.

Don't miss out on major issues. Subscribe now to Granta and save up to 40%.

Don't let your friends miss out either. One year gifts (4 issues) are only £21.95.

GRANTA

NO
STAMP
REQUIRED

Granta
FREEPOST
2-3 Hanover Yard
Noel Road
London
N1 8BR

NO
STAMP
REQUIRED

Granta
FREEPOST
2-3 Hanover Yard
Noel Road
London
N1 8BR

ago laid aside shovel and spanner, hammer and sickle for this greeting. Siberian frosts and the fire of the blast furnaces have hardened this skin. The delicate articulation of the finger joints has been restricted as if by a gouty stiffness. This clumsiness acquired through labour must make every heart beat faster that beats honestly on the side of working people.

By contrast, of course, the political body language of the *Heil* Hitler greeting was entirely appropriate to the class enemy: the slippery smooth fingers are pressed together and are slightly bent. Petty bourgeois pen-pusher's hands. The honest heavy hand of the class conscious worker does not get up to such tricks. Its vigorous grip signifies a feeling of grass-roots heartiness which is foreign to the decadent class and its intellectual parasites. All the effeminate elements hostile to the Party, the work-shy sceptics—the whole bourgeois rabble—betrayed itself by its limp body-language, even before it had uttered a single word.

At the moment of our handshake Gorbachev stiffened meaningfully. We were silent for a brief eternity. I even had the feeling that the habit of this rite of fraternal affection practised thousands upon thousands of times would propel Gorbachev into giving me a fraternal kiss. Elevating my cheeks to the ranks of Erich Honecker's and Jew-hater Yasser Arafat's. Fortunately this chalice passed me by. So we stood there, two survivors by the open grave of a fixed idea. Then we went on our way.

Translated from the German by Martin Chalmers.

WHAT KIND OF BOOK IS THIS?

Twenty-five encounters, or rendezvous, which, owing
to the reflection or the feeling they occasion, have
come to acquire some kind of extraordinary meaning.
This is both a collection of essays and a memoir; it is among
John Berger's most personal and revealing books.

KEEPING A RENDEZVOUS
John Berger

'Berger's mind travels the globe, and its range is astounding
. . one chapter begins with Giorgione's mysterious sixteenth-
century painting "La Tempesta", moves to a quotation from
Osip Mandelstam on Dante, then to a meditation on time that
involves references to Hegel, Marx, Camus, Goya, Stendhal
and Freud. Yet all this is done casually, in the manner of
a man thinking aloud or speaking to an intimate friend . .
KEEPING A RENDEZVOUS
should give only pleasure to
its readers' - Alison Lurie,
*New York Times
Book Review*

RUSSELL HOBAN
THE DEVIL'S KITCHEN

'Three hundred, five and seventy for this is quite a reasonable price,' the woman in the *Antiquitäten* assured me. My German isn't very good but I was able to follow most of what she said. She was young, had long yellow hair and the kind of wan prettiness that made me think of a little dark house by the road at dusk and a face seen from a car window. 'It isn't actually an antique—the furniture is maybe sixty years old or a little more but the pots and pans and implements are newer. These dolls' kitchens I collect but I have already three others at home and there is no space for so many.' She had two little yellow-haired sons in the shop; they looked away when I smiled at them.

Three hundred and seventy-five Deutschmarks was a little less than 132 pounds at the current rate of exchange, certainly a bargain. 'Where will you find space for it?' asked my wife, Gisela.

'I think I might get a story out of it,' I said. The dolls' kitchen seemed to be offering itself in some way. The human urge to replicate human and animal activities and their settings in miniature is something I've always wondered about. A clockwork figure of a porter pushing a trolley piled high with luggage; a tin rabbit ice-cream vendor on his ice-box tricycle; a cooker for a doll to prepare a meal on—such toys are strange and mysterious to me, they seem to be communicating more with the unseen than with the child for whom they are ostensibly intended. I still remember being given a beautiful stork that flew around and around a tin lighthouse; after a time it became too much for me and I had to put it away. I tend to feel uneasy with dolls' houses and dolls' rooms. The air in a room, the air between and around things—most people take it for granted but I never have; who knows what's moving in it? The silent conversation between tables and chairs, cupboards and shadows—who knows what's being said? And when everything is small like that, the air and the silence are concentrated in a particular way that isn't the safest thing in the world. No. So although I wanted this dolls' kitchen there was a certain amount of dread in my feelings about it.

With a photograph of it in front of me I'll now describe this artefact as precisely as I can because I want to make it perfectly clear that when I bought it there was no reason for me to think that it was anything more than what it appeared to be.

The kitchen had a back wall and two side walls angled out like the wings of a stage set. I suppose it was about two feet across the front; the walls were perhaps fourteen inches high and had white tiles up to the wainscot with little dark blue diamonds at the corners of each tile. Above the wainscot the walls were painted white. The moulding at the top of the walls and the pilasters at the edges of the two wings were light blue.

Against the left wall, as you viewed the kitchen from the front, was a high-backed yellow pine sideboard with two inset roundels decorated with little red flowers and green sprigs. All the furniture was yellow pine with the same floral motif. Ranged on the sideboard were a couple of jugs and a cup and a bowl, all this crockery made of wood. Above the sideboard hung a cleaver, two copper basins, a copper funnel and a copper saucepan with a long black handle. Next to the sideboard a laundry basket, then a corner cupboard.

On the back wall hung a wooden rack which held a rolling-pin, three long-handled wooden spoons and a wooden mallet. Under them stood a little table with a copper pot and a copper colander on it. Next came a dresser with closed shelves in its upper part. On top of the dresser stood a brass mortar and pestle and a deep copper pan.

On the right wall hung a tin frying-pan and under it a tin grater nearly half as long as the corner cupboard. Then a little hanging shelf with an egg-timer and a brown bottle on it. Then a white towel with a blue border. Under the little shelf stood a work table with a tin basin on it. In the basin was a mincing knife. Beside the basin lay a little wooden scoop. There was a chair by the work table and an aluminium bucket by the chair.

In the centre of the kitchen stood a coal stove with two deep aluminium pots on it. The white enamelled doors were outlined in dark blue. The stove-pipe ended in mid-air about four inches above the stove. Now I've described everything in that dolls' kitchen. No, I forgot the floor; the floor was black. The scales of things differed wildly—I've already mentioned the giant grater. The brass mortar on the shelf was as big as the bucket on the floor; the egg-timer was the size of the rolling-pin but held no more than eight seconds' worth of sand; the mincing knife could have been used as a scythe. Every single drawer and shelf was empty with a kind of hahaha emptiness. And that cut-off stove-pipe that went nowhere! I think about it now and shake my head.

Right, so that was the dolls' kitchen I bought in Celle, Gisela's home town in Lower Saxony. It's a town of carefully preserved half-timbered houses, many of them with seventeenth-century gilt lettering across their fronts, and it has a handsome white castle with a red pantiled roof and green domes in a beautiful green *Schlosspark* a few kilometres from Bergen-Belsen.

I took a Polaroid of the dolls' kitchen so I'd be sure to set it up properly and then the woman at the shop wrapped everything carefully in newspaper and put the whole affair in a big cardboard box. While the Polaroid was developing all dark and shadowy Gisela said, 'Is that a figure at the stove or what?'

'Where?'

'No, it's gone. It was nothing.'

We drove to the ferry at Bremerhaven and then home from Harwich and the whole time the dolls' kitchen, with its furniture and implements and the spaces and silences between them, waited to be reconstituted in our house in Fulham.

There's a table by the bay window in my study with two or three buried civilizations on it, so I cleared away some of that and set up the kitchen; it was the first thing I did before I even sorted the month's accumulation of mail. When I had it put together there it stood in the late-afternoon sunlight, everything in its wonted place but far from home. The shapes and the silences shook themselves like a dog coming out of the water and took up their duties, whatever they were, as before.

I watched it through the waning afternoon, I watched it at dusk. Beyond the window the trees of Eelbrook Common stood black against the purple sky; the red and green lights of the District Line became more intense as the evening deepened around them and trains with golden windows rumbled their passing on the shining iron of the rails. I didn't switch on any of the lights. The yellow street lamps picked out gleams and highlights on the pots and pans, and the rest of the little kitchen sank into shadows. It was like waiting for an unknown kind of egg to hatch. I watched it till half-past three in the morning and then I went to bed. Gisela woke up when I crept in beside her.

'What time is it?' she said.

I told her.

'What are you expecting to happen with that dolls' kitchen?'

'No idea. This is between me and it and it'll be whatever it'll be.'

'It's a dolls' kitchen. Isn't it possible that that's all it is? Sometimes I think you look for more in things than there is in them.'

'This is how I work, I can't help it.' We didn't say anything more but I could tell from the stillness beside me that she didn't go back to sleep for a while.

The next night I watched until four in the morning: nothing. I could feel it gathering itself and I knew it would happen on the third night.

The third night was a Sunday. There was no moon. The yellow street lamps reiterated the gleams and highlights on the little pots and pans. At three o'clock in the morning I heard, very faintly, the sound of a klaxon. It was far away but its suddenness was frightening. Immediately there followed the scuffling, shuffling tread of raggedly marching feet, unshod marching feet coming closer, closer, closer but I couldn't see anything. Then I heard tiny shrill voices singing the Horst Wessel song:

Die Fahne hoch, die Reihen fest geschlossen . . .
The banner high, the ranks tightly closed . . .

I smelled the unmistakable smell of dead rat and suddenly there were many tiny red eyes watching me from the shadows of the dolls' kitchen. I was shocked but not surprised—there are always rats around somewhere, alive or dead, large or small. '*Na?*' I said. '*Was machen Sie hier?*'

'*Was machen wir hier?*' they mocked. '*Wir warten auf dich, Töchterchen!* We wait for you, little daughter!'

I didn't care for that *dich*. 'You're getting altogether too familiar on very short acquaintance,' I said, 'and a bit confused as well. We are not *per du* and I'm not anyone's little daughter.' I could see them quite well now, dolls' rats in scale with the kitchen and somewhat misty and grey, as if they carried their own night and fog with them.

'But of course you are the little daughter,' they shrilled. 'Who keeps this kitchen is the little daughter, who keeps this kitchen is *du*, *du*, *du*, Sweetie!' It was awful the way their tiny mouths shaped the words.

'All right,' I said, eager for the story and wanting to move on to whatever was next, 'I'll be the little daughter and you'll call me *du*. Now what?'

Their eyes seemed brighter, their whiskers were twitching excitedly. 'Pardon?' they twittered, leaning forward. 'You must louder speak, we don't hear you.'

I was sitting at my desk in a swivel chair. I rolled closer to them and said it louder.

'Please,' they said, 'a little closer still. For us to see you isn't easy. We must the little daughter see.'

Trying not to breathe in their smell I brought my face still closer. Perhaps I overbalanced myself; suddenly the chair shot out from under me and I was in the kitchen with them and they weren't little compared to me as they should have been—we were all people-sized which made most of them bigger than I. They were in an advanced state of putrefaction: their fur was matted and stiff with dried blood; the entrails of many of them, wet with the juices of decay, were spilling out of gaping wounds; they were all squirming with maggots that glistened slickly in the yellow light of the street lamps.

There's nothing deader than a dead rat, especially active dead ones like these. The classic stench of them, together with the inverted V of their mouths and the look of their fingery little hands, seemed long familiar, part of one's unspoken reality. The stench was intensified proportionately with their increase in size and it combined with the smell of the yellow pine and the pots and pans in a way that made me grab the bucket just in time to vomit into it.

'No, no, Sweetie,' said one who appeared to be in charge. 'Here you don't do that, here you cook.'

'Oh yes,' I said, wiping my mouth with the towel, 'and with

168

what? There's no food whatever in this kitchen and the stove is
stone cold. And in any case I don't know how to cook anything
but eggs—boiled, scrambled, fried or poached. Or an omelette.
Have you got any eggs?' How long their teeth were, how red their
eyes in the fog in that kitchen!

'You must make *Eisbein mit Sauerkraut!*' shouted one.
'*Gruenkohl mit Brägenwurst!*' called another. '*Sauerbraten und
Klösse!*' '*Pellkartoffeln und Hering!*' '*Erbsensuppe!*' There was no
lack of suggestions.

'We know what He likes,' said the sergeant or whatever he
was. He said the He with a capital H. 'We bring you what to
burn in the stove and we bring you what to cook in the pot—all
is in order, Sweetie! Really!'

I don't want to talk about what they brought to burn in the
stove and cook in the pot—I think it may have been the same for
both. They brought and I cooked and that was how it started.
Regardless of the smell of the greasy black smoke that came out
of the cut-off stove-pipe and the mess that I stirred while I
looked away they insisted that I was preparing those traditional
dishes that He was so fond of; the pots were taken away full and
came back empty with compliments to the chef.

After a time the cooking part of the night seemed to be over.
'*Na?*' said the sergeant, bringing his face close to mine and
breathing heavily as he pinched my cheek and fondled my
bottom. 'You have learned well, little Sweetie.' I reached for the
rolling-pin and when he made a grab for me I hit him with it. All
that did was knock off some of the maggots without dampening
his ardour so I dropped the rolling-pin and got a good two-
handed grip on one of the handles of the great crescent-bladed
mincing knife and swung it as hard as I could. His head went
flying but one of the others caught it and threw it back to him.
The sergeant laughed as he stuck it back on and started pulling
down my trousers. His comrades now swarmed all over me and
although I cut off many heads with the mincing knife they stuck
them back on sideways, backwards, any old way and thought it a
great joke. I was quickly overpowered and in a very short time I
learned what it meant to be the little sweetie of that maggoty
platoon. Though dead, those rats had a great capacity for

enjoyment, even a sense of humour, some of them timing other punters with the egg-timer and making witty comments on their performance.

The party went on until dawn, at which time the distant klaxon sounded once more and I found myself alone in the dolls' kitchen. I put on my trousers and stepped uncertainly out on to the table. As I did so I reverted to my usual size and let myself down to the floor.

In the grey light of morning the dolls' kitchen showed no sign of the night's activity; everything was tidy and arranged in the same order as when I'd first set it up.

I took it out into the area by the dustbins and stamped on it several times. Then I got a hammer and smashed everything that was still unsmashed and dropped it all into the bin. That done, I went upstairs, had a long hot bath, did what I could for my sore places and dragged myself off to bed.

Gisela woke up. 'Where've you been all night?' she said.

'Mucking about.'

'Did you get a story out of it?'

'No.' Then I fell asleep like a stone dropping into a bottomless abyss.

I don't know what to think about what happened; maybe it says more about me than I want to know. Why was I so quick to say I'd be the little daughter and they could call me *du*? Was my hunger for a story the only reason? And how could I have stood there cooking what was in those pots on a stove that was burning what that stove burned? I try to console myself by remembering how hard I fought when they attacked me but of course by then it was too late.

Dracula is traditionally powerless to cross the threshold unless invited. In real life things are less clear-cut. Am I going to show this to Gisela? I think not.

GRANTA

PAWEL HUELLE
THE TABLE

'**O**h, that table!' my mother would shriek, 'I just can't stand it a moment longer! Other people have decent furniture.' She'd point at the round table where we ate our dinner every day. 'Do you really call that a table?' she'd ask.

My father would never rise to her goading; he'd withdraw into himself, and the room would fill with a heavy silence. Actually, the table wasn't all that bad. Its short leg was propped up with a wedge, and the gnarled surface could be covered with a tablecloth. My father had acquired the table in 1946 from Mr Polaske of Zaspa, when Mr Polaske packed his bags and took the last train west to Germany. In exchange, my father gave Mr Polaske a pair of army boots he'd got from a Soviet sergeant, who'd done a swap with him for a second-hand watch, but since the boots were not in mint condition, my father threw in some butter as well. Moved by this gesture, Mr Polaske gave my father a photograph from his family album. It showed two elegant men in suits, standing on what was then called Lange Brücke. I liked to look at this photograph, not out of interest in Mr Polaske and his brother, of whom I knew very little, but because in the background stretched a view that I'd sought in vain to rediscover on our own 'Long Harbour'. Dozens of fishing boats were moored at the Fish Market quay, the jetty was crowded with people buying and selling, and barges and steamships were sailing by on the Motława River, their funnels as tall as masts. The place was full of bustle and life. Lange Brücke looked like a real port, and although the signs above hotels, bars and tradesmen's counting houses were all in German, it was an attractive scene. It bore no resemblance to our own Long Harbour, rebuilt after the bombardment, the main features of which were a wasteland of administrative offices with red banners hanging on the walls, and the green thread of the Motława, constantly patrolled by a militia motorboat.

'It's a German table,' my mother would say adamantly. 'You should have hacked it to bits years ago. When I stop to think,' she'd go on, a little calmer now, 'that a Gestapo man used to sit at it and eat his eels after work, it makes me feel quite sick.'

My father would shrug his shoulders and hold out the

Opposite: Lange Brücke, Danzig

photograph of Mr Polaske.

'Look,' he'd say to my mother, 'is that a Gestapo man?' And then he'd tell the story of Mr Polaske, who was a Social Democrat and spent three years in Stutthof concentration camp because he didn't agree with Hitler. When our city was incorporated into the Reich in 1939 and changed its name from Gdańsk to Danzig, Mr Polaske made a point of not hanging a flag out of his window. It was after that they took him away.

'Well, his brother was a Gestapo man.' And with that my mother went into the kitchen, while my father, distressed that his audience had been reduced by half, told me the story of the other Mr Polaske, the brother, who immediately after the war had gone to Warsaw on behalf of the Gdańsk Germans to ask President Bierut if they could stay provided they signed a declaration of loyalty.

'And then,' my father's tale went on, 'President Bierut's moustache began to bristle, and he told Mr Polaske that the German Social Democrats had never erred on the side of good judgement, and that they had long since betrayed their class instinct—of which Comrade Stalin had written so wisely and comprehensively. "And any kind of request whatsoever"—President Bierut said, striking the desk top with his worker's fist—"is anti-state activity."' Mr Polaske's brother returned to Gdańsk and hanged himself in the attic of their home in Zaspa. 'And why do you think he did that?' my father asked loudly. 'After all, he could have gone back to Germany, like his brother.'

'He hanged himself,' my mother said as she came into the room with a steaming dish, 'because he was finally troubled by his conscience. If all Germans examined their consciences, they'd do just the same,' she added as she set the jacket potatoes on the table. 'They should all hang themselves, after what they've done.'

'And what about the Soviets?' my father exclaimed, shoving potato skins to the edge of his plate, 'what about them?'

I knew that the bickering was about to start. My mother had a deep-rooted and ineradicable fear of Germans, while my father reserved his venom for the compatriots of Fyodor Dostoevsky. An invisible borderline now ran across Mr Polaske's table, and it separated the two of them, just like in 1939, when the land of their childhood, scented with apples, halva and a wooden pencil case with crayons rattling in it, was ripped in half like a piece of canvas, with the silver thread of the River Bug glittering down the middle.

'I saw them,' my father said, as he gulped down the white potato flesh, 'I saw them . . . ' What he meant, of course, was the march-past in the little town where the two armies met. 'They raised the dust to the very heavens,' my father said, helping himself to more crackling, 'and they marched abreast in step, taking turns to sing in German and then in Russian, but you could hear the Russian louder because the Soviets had sent a whole regiment—the Germans sent only two companies.'

'The Germans were worse,' my mother interrupted, 'because they had no human feelings.'

I didn't like these conversations; the strong flavour of broth or the fragrant aroma of horseradish sauce would be infused with the thunder of cannon-fire or the clatter of a train carrying people off to a slow or instant death. I didn't like it when they argued about such things. I used to think, as I forced down my jacket potatoes or cheese-filled *pirozhki*, that if it weren't for Mr Polaske and his table, my parents would be chatting about a Marilyn Monroe film, or this year's strawberry crop, or the latest launching at the Lenin shipyard which Premier Cyrankiewicz had attended. Mr Polaske's table was like a persistent toothache. Whenever the pain eased, they'd be seized by an irresistible urge to touch the sore spot and provoke the throbbing agony again.

Then, in addition to its lame leg and blistered veneer came woodworm. It gave my mother sleepless nights. In the morning she'd be tired and bad-tempered.

'Do something,' she'd say to my father. 'I just can't stand it any longer! Those are German weevils. Soon they'll attack the dresser and the cupboard, because they are insatiable, like everything German.'

Often I imagined Mr Polaske rubbing his hands together, laughing to himself somewhere in Hamburg or Munich. He'd have eaten the butter and thrown out the Soviet boots yet we were still suffering with his table; it was like an alien member of the household, always getting in everybody's way, impossible to get rid of. Why should Mr Polaske want revenge on us? We'd done him no harm. We weren't even living in his house, which was now occupied by some high-up Party official. Could he have wished us ill simply because we were Polish? For hours I'd gaze at the photograph, in which Long Harbour looked like a real port, and I'd count the funnels of the steamships winding their way along the Motlawa River. The table, meanwhile, seemed to get bigger, swelling to impossible dimensions within the small confines of the room.

At last the inevitable happened. As my mother set down a tureen full of soup, the wedge came loose from beneath the short leg, and the table staggered like a wounded beast. Beetroot soup splashed across my father's shirt and trousers.

'Oh!' exclaimed my mother and clasped her hands together in rapture. 'Didn't I say this would happen? Didn't I predict a catastrophe?'

My father didn't say a single word. He replaced the wedge, ate his second course, sat out the cherry blancmange in silence, and only after dessert, with a cigarette between his teeth, did he go down to the cellar for his saw and tape-measure. Soon he was leaning over the table, squinting first with one eye, then the other, like a surgeon preparing to operate. My father, who was handy at repairs, was having trouble coping with Mr Polaske's table. Or rather with the table's uneven legs. After each pruning it would turn out that one of them—each time it was a different one—was just a fraction shorter that the rest. My father refused to admit defeat: possessed by the Fury of perfection, or maybe of German pedantry, he went on and on, shortening the table legs, until at last on the floor, beside heaps of wood and sawdust, lay the top of Mr Polaske's table, like a great brown shield. My mother's eyes glittered with emotion. Nothing could restrain my father from completing the task. The snarling saw ripped into the table-top; my mother held her breath, and then cried:

'Well, at last!'

Mr Polaske's table was only good for burning now.

My father took the bits of wood down to the cellar, my mother swept up the sawdust, and I had a feeling in my bones that this wasn't the end of the matter: our real troubles were only just beginning.

Next day we ate dinner in the kitchen. It was cramped and uncomfortable and smelled of fried herrings.

'We'll have to buy a new table,' said my mother, 'a bit smaller than the old one perhaps, though it should still be round. And then some new chairs,' she added, drifting into the realms of fantasy, 'with plush covers!'

My father was silent.

After dinner we took the tram to the furniture shop. The salesman threw his arms wide in a gesture of helplessness, smiled tellingly and said all they had, we could see before us: nothing but triangular tables.

'It's the latest model,' he said, pointing out the geometric shape. 'Experimental, it is.'

'What about round ones?' asked my mother. 'Aren't there any round ones?'

The salesman explained that this year's central plan had already been fulfilled, and that while of course there would be some more round tables, they would not arrive until January or February. My father gave an acid smile, since we were bang in the middle of May. My mother, meanwhile, walked about among the triangular tables, touching their surfaces in disbelief and horror. Light streamed into the shop through the dust-caked window, illuminating her chestnut hair with a soft halo, giving her a melancholy allure.

Once outside, she insisted we go to another shop. But the blind Fate of the central plan hovered over all the furniture shops in town. The only non-triangular table, brought out at her express demand from a murky storeroom, turned out to be rectangular, very long and narrow, and utterly unsuitable for our room. I wondered if Mr Polaske could imagine this scene. After a few hours, we got home exhausted, while his table went on hanging in our midst, like a spectral cloud of sawdust.

'At the end of the day,' my father commented, 'we could always order a table. It'll be dearer, but'—here he paused meaningfully and raised his finger aloft like a preacher—'in view of the central plan there is no other way out.'

This made sense. But we soon found out that of the five carpenter's workshops in the neighbourhood, three had closed down long ago. Their owners, ruined by high taxes, now worked at the state factory, fulfilling the central plan. The fourth, which belonged to a Mrs Rupiejek, the widow of a carpenter from Wilno, was in the process of liquidation. And the fifth had been turned into a private business, making very fine coffins which—for now, at least—were exempt from central planning.

We still had no table.

My father's ephemeral, poetic improvisations were doomed to failure. He balanced the ironing board on twin chests, then knocked something resembling a table-top together in the cellar. Finally he had the idea of placing an advertisement in the morning paper —'Wanted: second-hand table. If it's round, I'll buy it.' This notion seemed particularly awful to my mother. It was a second-hand table which had caused all this trouble in the first place! And so our final hope lay with Mr Gorzki, who without shop sign or permit, did a bit of carpentry on the side, using materials pilfered from the shipyard. He also drank, as if he were a sailor, not a carpenter. Anyway, he took a large deposit from my father and promised to make the table within a week. A first-rate round table. My mother was very pleased, although my law-abiding father was a little uncomfortable.

'If I'm aware,' he'd ask loudly each evening, 'that he's going to make us a table out of stolen wood, can that be right? Is that really honest?'

My mother was a pragmatist.

'Who's it stealing from? It all belongs to the state. Every last bit of it,' she said, describing a vast circle in the air, like destiny itself.

However, destiny spoke even more conclusively through Mr Gorzki. The carpenter did not complete his drinking on the previous Sunday evening, but prolonged it through the whole of Monday. He resumed it on Tuesday, sustained it on Wednesday, and expertly added impetus on Thursday, until at last he'd pulled through to Friday, where, after midnight, Saturday and Sunday lay in thirsty anticipation. On Monday my father and I reached Mr Gorzki's shed, where he received us sitting on the earthen floor amid bottles and scattered tools. His face shone with a mixture of gloom and ecstasy. He raised his head, guffawed throatily and croaked out the same old sentence over and over: 'I know! I know!'

My father went purple.

'Where's my money?' he shouted. 'Where's our table? Give me back my deposit!' His voice cracked. 'Give it back this instant!'

But even I could see that my father's shouting was purely for the sake of form. It no longer had anything to do with Mr Gorzki who, right now, before our very eyes, was cutting the threads that tied him to the world of cause and effect.

From then on Mr Polaske began to visit our flat. He'd knock very gently at the door, greet my father with a nod and then silently walk round his table, which was by now entirely invisible. He'd put down gifts on it—a packet of coffee, some chocolate, a box of English tea—and then he'd slip away quietly, to avoid encountering my mother. The presents looked odd hanging in mid-air, and whenever I reached out to touch them they vanished, just like Mr Polaske. I never discussed these visits with my father, who was growing more and more distracted. It was possible that he hadn't even noticed the fleeting presence of our guest. But I wondered what, for instance, would be the result of an encounter between my mother and Mr Polaske? And what if he made an unexpected appearance at the kitchen table? But nothing like that happened.

One day my father came home from work particularly excited.

'I've got it!' he cried from the doorway. 'I've got us a table at last!'

My mother looked out of the window.

'I don't see the van,' she noted drily.

My father took a slip of paper from his pocket and announced that what we had to do was go to Mr Kasper, who makes the kind of table they used to make before the war—good and solid and round, or oval, or elliptical, whatever the customer's order. And this was the secret of the enterprise: Mr Kasper accepted commissions only from reliable people, on a personal recommendation. My father flourished the note in the air like a winning lottery ticket and added that Kasper the carpenter lived in Zulawy, on the other side of the Vistula.

The carpenter's house looked like a little wooden box with a small porch and fancy attic windows. It was submerged in the greenery of ancient willow trees and shrubs. We stood in the deserted yard, looking around us uncertainly. Eventually a wrinkle-faced woman of indeterminate age came out towards us from the garden which extended behind the house.

'Who is it you want?' she asked.

'Mr Kasper,' said my father, smiling. 'We have business to do with him.'

'It's not Kasper, it's Kaspar,' said the woman.

She looked at us with suspicion, or maybe just indifference; anyway she didn't say anything else, and we went on standing there, in the close, motionless mid-day air.

'Is he at home?' my father asked after a long pause.

'At home?' the woman said indignantly. 'You'll have to go down the path till you get to the cattle round-up. That's where he is!' And she swiftly turned away, the hem of her apron flapping, and disappeared among the bushes.

'Come on then,' I heard my father sigh. 'We'll find him.'

We followed the cobblestones, and then a sandy path, which threw up a thick dust that stung our throats, made our eyes smart and felt gritty between our teeth. We were guided along by hoofmarks.

'It can't be far now,' said my father.

The path was covered with animal dung, and we had to be careful not to sink our feet into cow shit. It was blazing hot, and if it hadn't been for my father, I'd have turned back. Even the sight of a windmill, with useless stumps for blades, did not arouse my curiosity.

At last we reached an open space. A bunker-like building stood in the middle, its walls made of cement. It had no proper windows, only a strip of small skylights running just beneath a flat, board-like roof. A shabby yellow inn sign announced that we were standing before the Boar's Head. Inside, several men were sitting at wobbly little tables.

'There's no beer left,' the portly barman cried. 'They've swilled the lot already.'

The strong smell of tobacco smoke, urine, sweat and soured

alcohol engulfed us like a mist. My father explained to the barman who we were looking for, while I scrutinized the customers' faces. They were tanned and deep-furrowed, all wearing the same expression, as if staring into space.

Mr Kaspar was in the corner, almost invisible in the semi-darkness, smoking the stump of a cigar. There was no empty tankard on his table. Leaning forward, my father took the note out of his pocket, placed it down like a visiting card and whispered the story of the table to Mr Kaspar, who listened in silence, smoking the last of his cigar.

Mr Kaspar rose and we followed him out of the bar. He had a piglet on a bit of rope. He mentioned that official inspectors had been round today, which was why he hadn't sold his pig, and had sat waiting in the bar. God knows what he was waiting for—the end of the world, perhaps, or maybe better days. A few days before he'd dreamed that a grown-up man and a little boy had knocked at his door with good news. The dream had put him in an excellent mood. My father glanced discreetly at his watch; the last narrow-gauge railway train was leaving in an hour's time.

'Doesn't life disturb you?' said the carpenter, suddenly gripping my father's arm, 'What is it beside eternity? A brief moment, nothing but a speck of dust! Where are we going? And where have we come from?'

'Yes, indeed,' said my father, 'but,' and he hesitated, 'will you make the table? It's extremely important to us.'

We had reached the house. Between the blackcurrant bushes and some thick clumps of peonies, an uncommon bustle was underway. The wrinkle-faced woman had brought out plates and cutlery, while Mr Kaspar, as if he hadn't heard my father, set out wicker chairs round a small stone table. Before my father had a chance to say anything further, we were sitting down to soup with the large golden eyes of egg yolks floating in it, followed by a joint of meat. After our meal, Mr Kaspar brought a jug up from the cellar; from it he filled chunky glasses with dark, aromatic juniper beer.

'The real art of it,' he said, raising his glass to eye level, 'relies on not adding too many of these little berries—and on picking them at the right time of day, early in the afternoon, when they've been warmed up by the sun and are giving off their juice.'

I watched my father as he took long draughts of the cloudy liquid. His face gradually brightened, taking on an unusual shine, and the two gentlemen began to spin the yarn of reminiscences. My father related how in 1945 he'd paddled across the Vistula to Gdańsk in an old canoe, because he didn't have any documents and was afraid of railway stations and places frequented by Soviet patrols. Mr Kaspar spoke of a long train journey which had ended abruptly when German saboteurs blew up the tracks not far from here. He'd had to find a place to stay and walked through one village after another—the only sound the occasional creak of shutters—unable to stop because nothing he saw matched the city he had left behind him, the most beautiful city in the world, a city of churches and synagogues, near gentle hills and pine forests, the city of his childhood, youth and war, which was now under Bolshevik power.

'And that's the power of Satan,' said Mr Kaspar pensively. 'The land of darkness and cruel oppression.'

Mr Kaspar poured more juniper-scented beer into the glasses. A light early-evening mist floated on the air, shrilly whistling swallows were swooping under the eaves, and my father, as if he'd forgotten all about the narrow-gauge railway and the table, said that the Lord God must long since have lost interest in us, for a world like this one to be possible.

'Oh, no!' Mr Kaspar snorted. 'We can never be sure what lies ahead. And anyway, has the world really deserved a better fate?'

The leaves began to rustle and a light breeze blew across the garden from the river. Mr Kaspar began to tell my father about a storm which one spring had broken down the dams and demolished the floodgates. The sea had invaded all the way up to here, to the foot of Mr Kaspar's house.

'Just imagine,' he said, leaning over my father, 'I cast my rod out of the window and reeled in a . . . Can you guess?'

'A catfish!' cried my father. 'There must be enormous catfish in these canals!'

'It was a seven-kilo cod!' recalled Mr Kaspar delightedly. 'And when the water had been standing there a bit longer, I could draw in netfuls of herrings!'

I'd been given a couple of mouthfuls of beer and could feel
the little bubbles of juniper starting to spin in my head. Without
being noticed, I left the veranda and plunged into the
undergrowth, walking along paths overgrown with burdock, the
strong scent of peonies swirling in the air.

'*We're the men of the First Brigade!*' my father's voice soared
high above the trees.

'*With a rifle fusillade!*' Mr Kaspar chimed in, and then they
sang on in chorus: '*On to the pyre we cast our lot! On to the pyre!*' I
heard them toast Marshal Pilsudski, and then there was a sound of
breaking glass.

Later on I caught sight of them on a wide lane running
between the apple trees. They were strolling towards the river.

'Of course I'll help you,' my father was saying. 'Mind you,
I've never done it before.'

'Yes, yes,' the carpenter replied, 'I always wait until after
dusk,' because it's not a simple job. You've got to be careful!'

The red disc of the moon was rising in the sky as the two
gentlemen disappeared into a large shed, closely planted
round with forsythia and hazel. I sat down nearby at the
water's edge. Further down the river, among the reeds and rushes,
I could see the wreck of a barge, which had been driven into the
bank like a mighty wedge. The air stood still, and I thought of Mr
Polaske. Might he pay a visit to our flat while my father and I
were at Mr Kaspar's? The last narrow-gauge railway train had left
hours ago, and my mother was sure to be in our neighbour's flat
by now, calling the police and the hospitals to confirm her worst
forebodings. What if she met Mr Polaske in the dark stairwell,
silent and pensive in his long overcoat? Or worse still, what if she
saw him in the flat itself?

There was no sound coming from the shed, nor was the
faintest ray of light peeping through the closed shutter, although
I noticed a grey thread of smoke seeping from a small chimney.
Then the air was suddenly pierced by an unearthly scream.

I was paralysed. I stood on the riverbank, staring at the black
outline of the shed. After a few moments I crept up to it and
gingerly pushed the door ajar. Through the chink I could see Mr

Kaspar in a white apron splattered with blood. With both hands he had raised a big chopper, and my father was shouting loudly say, 'No, no—not like that!' The axe struck something soft which was lying on the table, and blood spouted in all directions. Mr Kaspar, wiping the red streaks from his face, said, 'Yes, maybe it really hasn't all flowed out as it should.'

A fire was blazing in a large oven. Mr Kaspar put down the chopper and, knife in hand, began cutting up red and pink steaks of the meat that was hanging from hooks around the room. Nearby on the floorboards lay the piglet's head, its open eyes gazing at me. The two men rinsed the cuts of meat in bowls, shoving some into earthenware pots and smearing others with a sort of powder, then hanging them up on an iron rail in the depths of the oven.

'We should be done by morning,' said Mr Kaspar, putting down his long, broad knife. 'It's lucky that you came today. My wife can't bear the sight of this.'

My father wiped his hands, and from a crystal decanter which stood on the shelf, he poured ruby-red liquid, thicker and darker than blood, into two glasses.

'Your wife isn't very talkative,' said my father, wiping his mouth. 'But she's got an unusual accent. Pomeranian, but different, somehow.'

'You noticed?' said the carpenter, setting to work again. 'You did notice, didn't you?'

Mr Kaspar began to tell of how he dreamed of *them* at night, of how he saw *them* passing through the entrance to the camps, dressed in black cloaks, and there, up above, the Lord God opening the gates and welcoming them in with a smile. They, who tilled the land and dug out canals, built floodgates, erected windmills, sang psalms and hymns, and would never, on any account, take up arms.

'They . . . ?' asked my father hesitantly, as he set the oven door ajar.

Mr Kaspar gently sighed. He told him about the Mennonites, of whom hardly a trace was left, and of the house he had entered at the end of the war, thinking it would be empty like the rest. But after two whole days had passed he saw a pair of shining eyes up in the deepest corner of the attic. They were her eyes, the eyes of a Mennonite, the last on the earth.

'Ah, yes,' said my father.

I stood in the doorway gazing at the ruby-red liquid in the crystal decanter and the cuts of meat hanging on hooks, while Mr Kaspar went on with his story. He had stared into those eyes and known at once that they understood him, although for months he had been unable to explain to her exactly where he had come from, and why he had taken the train so far westwards. He couldn't describe his city to her, for she—at this point Mr Kaspar put the bowl aside and reached for a bag of cereal—she knew only one city, the one she used to sail to for the market; it was completely different from his own. And now it had been burned to the ground.

'But even the ruins looked uncanny,' said my father, holding up the intestine for the carpenter to stuff. 'When I paddled my canoe out on to the Motlawa River and first caught sight of the ruins from a distance, the whole place looked like a city on the moon.'

Mr Kaspar shook his head and tied up the stuffed intestine with some fine string. At that precise moment my father looked up and saw me standing in the doorway.

'Aren't you in bed yet?' he cried in amazement. 'What on earth's the time?' But Mr Kaspar gestured to him to be silent, asked him to keep an eye on the fire—since there's nothing more ruinous for cured ham than an uneven stream of smoke—and set off across the garden leading me along the path towards the house.

'What's happening about the table?' I asked timidly.

Mr Kaspar replied that it would all be fine, that there was a right time for everything.

In the distance, from the direction of the river, several voices were hoarsely crooning: 'And then you'll pity me a little, and then you'll give me a kiss, my pretty!'

'That's the Ukrainians from the collective farm across the river,' explained the carpenter. 'They drink, they sing, they have a sad time.

'Do you know why they're sad?' he then asked unexpectedly.

We stood in front of the house, watching the long shadows of the trees as they spread across the garden paths. I didn't know why.

'It's because of the moon,' said Mr Kaspar. 'When it's full, they drink and sing. Even in winter. A long time ago, perhaps ten years, they walked across the ice to this side and set the shed on fire. The moon seemed bigger then, as it always does when there's snow on the ground.'

I wanted to talk to Mr Kaspar about our table. My father certainly wouldn't have told him about the Polaske brothers from Zaspa. But the carpenter hurried away before I had the chance, vanishing like a shadow among the trees.

The wrinkle-faced woman took me up to a room in the attic and showed me my made-up bed. But I wasn't sleepy. As soon as I heard her footsteps on the stairs, I went up to the window and opened it wide. The roof of the shed, the trees and the bright ribbon of the river were all clearly visible in the moonlight. Only the wreck of the barge was lost from sight somewhere round a bend among the reeds and rushes. On the far shore the Ukrainians had lit a bonfire. I could see their figures weaving in and out of its light, and I was sorry I couldn't hear their song.

Suddenly I was seized with longing to know everything. Where does the river flow to? Where was Mr Kaspar's city? Why weren't the Mennonites willing to take up arms? Did they really all go to heaven? I'd forgotten all about Mr Polaske, my mother and the round table, for which we'd come over the pontoon bridge across the Vistula.

I noticed a wardrobe with carved legs and opened the door. Inside I found a hat. It was black, with a huge brim and felt edges. I put it on and stood in front of the mirror. I could see my reflected face, obscured by the brim's shadow, my eyes and lips barely visible. And then the hat seemed to grow larger. It got bigger and bigger. I seemed to be growing too, until I was as tall as my father and as broad-shouldered as Mr Kaspar. I crossed the moonlit garden to the river and stepped aboard the barge. I guided my ship through locks and floodgates, until at last I sailed out on to the Motlawa River and dropped anchor at Long Harbour amid the throng of masts, chimneys and ensigns. I asked the Ukrainians to unload. Sacks of grain, baskets full of apples and plums, barrels with live fish swimming in them, pieces of cloth scented with summer and with herbs, several pound tubs of butter—all this made its way from the hold on to the jetty. The Ukrainians crooned plaintively as they worked, a song in which a Mr Potocki, '*that son of a dog, betrayed Lithuania, Poland and all Ukraine.*' Although I didn't understand all the words, I listened as if they were a familiar refrain expressing inconsolable yearning and anger.

The black hat gradually regained its depth and sharpness in the mirror, when suddenly I caught sight of a candle flame. Above the broad brim the woman's wrinkled face appeared. She was standing behind me, holding a candlestick, and the hem of her dressing gown fell to her ankles. I didn't know when she'd entered the room or for how long she'd been watching me at the mirror. Could she have seen me on the barge? Tears were pouring down her cheeks. With a delicate movement she took the hat from my head and turned it in her hands.

The wrinkle-faced woman stared into the blackness of the hat. She was lost in thought. Then she left the room, clutching the black brim with both hands.

I blew out the candle. The starched bedlinen enfolded me with soothing coolness, and yet I was burning hot, as if I were standing by the oven in the shed, where Mr Kaspar and my father, busy with their illegal butchery, had forgotten all about the passage of time and the world outside.

I didn't exchange a single word with the wrinkle-faced woman the next morning, as the two men discussed the particulars of the order over a breakfast of smoked bacon and black pudding: diameter of the table top, the leg height and the colour of the veneer.

I didn't tell my father about the black hat as we travelled by narrow-gauge railway along the River Tuja past overgrown canals and closed-down locks. Nor did I tell him later as we streaked across the pontoon bridge over the Vistula in a sky-blue bus, nor even when the brick church-towers loomed ahead in the suburbs of Long Gardens.

As my father unwrapped some juniper-scented ham from a greasy piece of paper, and my mother nursed a migraine with a damp towel round her head, they each let fly with words such as 'duty', 'table', 'thoughtlessness' and 'opportunity'. I looked at their angry faces and in my thoughts I was with the wrinkle-faced woman: I would never forget her.

A week later there was a knock at our door and some strange men carried Mr Kaspar's table into the living-room. It was round, with a walnut veneer, and utterly enraptured my mother. The squabbling and bickering stopped completely, and that day dinner went on for ages, just as if Grandma Maria had come to visit us.

And once the chestnut trees along our street were in bloom, and I was bent over Mr Kaspar's table, slogging away at the first letters of my ABC, getting to know the fortunes of Ala, who has a cat, Mr Polaske knocked at our door. He was bashful and awkward and told us how he'd found our address and what troubles he'd had with his visa and with the officials at the Ministry of Foreign Affairs. He sat at Mr Kaspar's table and took out some coffee, cocoa, chocolate and a tin of English tea as he talked about his journey and how very happy he was to be here.

'Will you have dinner with us?' asked my mother, but Mr Polaske was in a hurry to get to his hotel. He said thank you, apologized and left quickly, bid farewell by my father in the doorway.

'He didn't notice the table,' said my father.

But I wasn't so sure. The presents which he left did not disappear this time. I turned the pages of the primer. Ala went to school. Father went to work. Mother cooked the dinner. The workers smelted steel. The miners extracted coal. The pilot flew over the motherland. The Vistula flowed to the Baltic. The woman took away the black hat. The Mennonites went straight to heaven. Mr Polaske sold a table, and Mr Kaspar made a new one.

'What are you reading? He's making it up, isn't he?' asked my mother.

'Yes, he is,' said my father, lighting a cigarette and placing the palm of his hand on the table top as the light skimmed across it, 'it's all made up. Every single world of it!'

I gazed at the trail of smoke wafting up towards the ceiling. From then on time went by differently, and only I knew why.

Translated from the Polish by Antonia Lloyd-Jones

GRANTA

HARUKI MURAKAMI
LEDERHOSEN

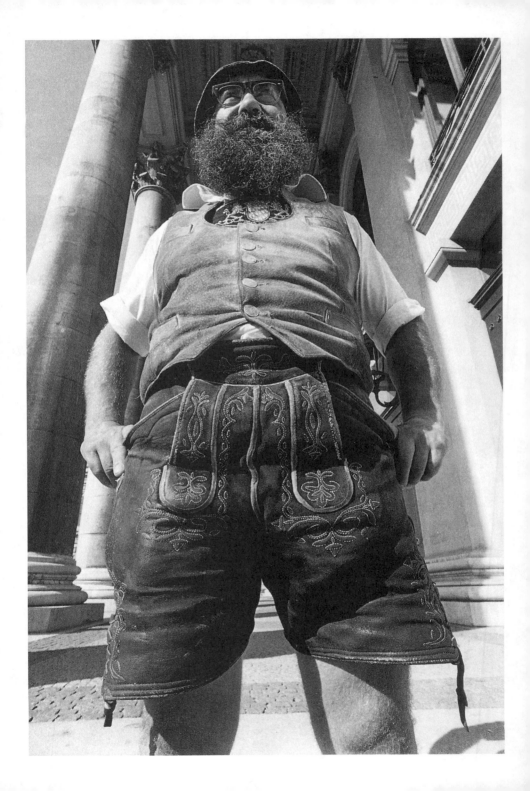

'**M**other dumped my father,' a friend of my wife was saying one day, 'all because of a pair of shorts.'

I had to ask. 'A pair of shorts?'

'I know it sounds strange,' she said, 'because it is a strange story.'

My wife's friend is a large woman; her height and build are almost the same as mine. She tutors electric organ, but most of her free time she divides between swimming, skiing and tennis, so she's trim and always tanned. I like sports, but you might call her a fanatic. On days off, she puts in a morning run before heading to the local pool; then at two or three in the afternoon it's tennis, followed by aerobics. I don't mean to suggest she's obsessive about things. Quite the contrary, she's really quite relaxed. Only she's driven, her body—and very likely her spirit—craves vigorous activity, relentless as a comet.

Which may have something to do with why she's unmarried. She's had affairs—the woman may be a little on the large side, but she is beautiful—she's been proposed to, even agreed to take the plunge. But each time some problem has come up and everything has fallen through.

My wife says she's unlucky. I sympathize but I'm not in total agreement with my wife on this. True, luck may cast patches of shadows over parts of a person's life but where there's a will—much less a will strong enough to swim thirty lengths or run twenty kilometres—there's a way to overcome almost any trouble. I believe her heart was never set on marrying. So she keeps on tutoring electric organ, devoting every free moment to sport, falling regularly, unluckily, in and out of love.

It's a rainy Sunday afternoon and she's arrived two hours earlier than expected. My wife is still out shopping.

'Forgive me,' she apologizes. 'I took a raincheck on today's tennis, which left me two hours free. I'd have been bored out of my mind being alone at home, so I just thought . . . Am I interrupting anything?'

Not at all, I say. I didn't feel quite in the mood to work and was just sitting around, cat on my lap, watching a video. I show her in, go to the kitchen and make coffee. Two cups, for

Photo: Hulton Deutsch Collection

watching the last twenty minutes of *Jaws*. Of course, we've both seen the movie before—probably more than once—so neither of us is particularly riveted but we watch it anyway. When it ends there is still no sign of my wife. So we chat for a while: sharks, seaside, swimming . . . Still no wife. We go on talking. I like this woman well enough, but after an hour our lack of things in common becomes obvious. She's my wife's friend not mine.

I'm already thinking about popping in the next video when she suddenly brings up the story of her parents' divorce. I can't fathom the connection—at least to my mind there's no link between swimming and her parents splitting up—but I expect a reason is where you find it.

‘They weren't really shorts,' she says. 'They were lederhosen.'

‘You mean those hiking pants the Germans wear? With the shoulder straps?'

‘That's right. Father wanted a pair of lederhosen as a souvenir gift. Well, Father's pretty tall. He might even have looked good in them. But can you picture a Japanese wearing lederhosen?'

I'm still not any closer to the story. I have to ask, what were the circumstances behind her father's request for these souvenir lederhosen?

‘Oh, I'm sorry. I'm always telling things out of order. Stop me if things don't make sense,' she says.

‘OK,' I say.

‘Mother's sister was living in Germany and she invited Mother for a visit. Something she'd always been meaning to do. Of course, Mother can't speak German, and she'd never been abroad, but it'd been ages since she'd seen my aunt. So Mother approached Father, how about taking ten days off and going to Germany, the two of us? Father's work wouldn't allow it, so Mother went alone.'

‘That's when your father asked for the lederhosen, I take it?'

‘Right,' she says. 'Mother asked what he wanted her to bring back, and Father said lederhosen.'

‘OK so far.'

Her parents were reasonably close. They didn't argue until all hours of the night; her father didn't storm out of the house and not come home for days on end, though apparently there had been rows more than once over him and other women.

'Not a bad man, a hard worker, but kind of a skirt-chaser,' she explains matter-of-factly. He's no relation of hers, the way she's talking. For a second I almost think her father is dead. But no, I'm told, he's alive and well.

Her mother extended her ten days in Germany to nearly a month and a half, with hardly a word back to Tokyo, and when she finally did return to Japan, she stayed with another sister of hers in Osaka. She never did come back home.

Neither daughter nor father could understand what had happened. Until then, when there had been marital difficulties, the mother had always been the patient one; family had always come first and she was selflessly devoted to her daughter. So when she didn't come around, didn't even make the effort to call, it was beyond their comprehension. They made phone calls to the aunt's house in Osaka, repeatedly, but they could hardly get her to come to the phone, much less to admit her intentions.

In mid-September, two months after returning to Japan, her mother called home and told her husband, 'You will be receiving the necessary papers for divorce. Please sign them and send them back to me.' Would she care to explain, her husband asked, her reasons? 'I've lost all love for you—in any way, shape or form.' Was there no room for discussion? Sorry, none, absolutely none.

Telephone negotiations dragged on for the next two or three months, but her mother did not back down an inch and finally her father consented to the divorce. He was in no position to force the issue, his own track record being what it was, and anyway he always tended to give in.

'All this came as a shock,' she tells me. 'Not just the divorce—I'd imagined my parents splitting up many times—if it had just been that I wouldn't have got so upset. The problem wasn't Mother dumping Father; Mother was dumping me too. That's what hurt.'

I nodded.

'Up until that point, I'd always taken Mother's side and

Mother would always stand by me. And yet here was Mother throwing me out with Father, like so much garbage, and not a word of explanation. It hit me so hard, I wasn't able to forgive Mother for the longest time. I wrote her who knows how many letters asking her to set things straight but she never answered my questions, never even said she wanted to see me.'

It wasn't until three years later that she actually saw her mother. At a family funeral of all places. By then, the daughter was living on her own—she'd moved out in her sophomore year, when her parents divorced—and now she had graduated and was tutoring electric organ Meanwhile, her mother was teaching English at a prep school.

She hadn't been able to talk to her own daughter because she hadn't known what to say. 'I myself couldn't tell where things were going,' she said, 'but the whole thing started over that pair of shorts.'

My wife's friend had never wanted to speak to her mother ever again, but curiosity got the better of her. 'Shorts?' In their mourning clothes, mother and daughter went into a nearby coffee shop and ordered iced tea. She had to hear this—pardon the expression—short story.

The shop that sold the lederhosen was in a small town an hour away by train from Hamburg.

'All the Germans I know say this is the place. The craftsmanship is good, and the prices aren't so expensive,' said her sister.

So Mother boarded a train to buy her husband his souvenir lederhosen. In her train compartment sat a middle-aged German couple, who conversed with her in halting English.

'I go now to buy lederhosen for souvenir,' Mother said.

'Vat shop you go to?' the couple asked.

Mother said the name of the shop, and the middle-aged German couple chimed in together, 'Zat is ze place, *ja*. It is ze best.'

Hearing this, Mother felt very confident.

It was a delightful early summer afternoon. A brook flowed through the middle of the town, its banks lush and green.

Cobblestone streets led in all directions, and there were cats everywhere. Mother stepped into a café for a bite of *Käsekuchen* and a coffee.

She was on her last sip of coffee and playing with the shop cat when the owner came over to ask what brought her to their little town.

'Lederhosen,' she said. Whereupon the owner pulled out a pad of paper and drew a map showing the location of the shop.

How wonderful it was to travel by oneself, she thought as she walked along the cobblestones. In fact, this was the first time in her fifty-five years that she had travelled alone. She had not once been lonely or afraid or bored. Every scene that met her eyes was fresh and new; everyone she met was friendly. What she had held near and dear until then—husband and home and daughter—were on the other side of the earth.

She found the lederhosen shop without any problem. It was a tiny old guild shop. It didn't have a big sign for tourists, but inside she could see scores of lederhosen. She opened the door and walked in.

Two old men worked in the shop. They spoke in a whisper as they took down measurements and scribbled them into a notebook. From behind a curtain the monotone of sewing machines could be heard.

'*Darf ich Ihnen helfen, Madame?*' the larger of the two old men addressed Mother.

'I want to buy lederhosen,' she responded in English.

'For Madame?' he asked.

'No, I buy for my husband in Japan.'

'*Ach so,*' said the old man, 'your husband, he is not here viss you?'

'No, I say already, he is in Japan,' she replied.

'Ziss make problem,' the old man chose his words with care. 'Ve do not make article for customer who not exist.'

'My husband exist,' Mother said with confidence.

'*Ja,* of course, of course,' the old man responded hastily. 'Excuse my not good English. Vat I vant say, if your husband not exist here, ve cannot sell ze lederhosen.'

'Why?' Mother asked, perplexed.

'Is store policy. *Ist unser Prinzip.* Ve must see ze lederhosen how it fit customer, ve alter very nice, only zen ve sell. Over one hundred years ve are in business, ve build reputation on ziss policy.'

'But I spend half a day to come from Hamburg to buy your lederhosen.'

'Very sorry, Madame,' said the old man, looking very sorry indeed. 'Ve make no exception. Ziss vorld is very uncertain vorld. Trust is difficult sink to earn but easy sink to lose.'

Mother sighed and stood in the doorway. The taller old man explained the situation to the smaller old man, who nodded sadly, *ja, ja.* Despite their great difference in size, the two old men wore identical expressions.

'How about this,' Mother proposed. 'I will find a man just like my husband and bring him here, the man puts on the lederhosen, you alter them and sell the lederhosen to me.'

The first man looked her in the face, aghast.

'But Madame, zat is against the rule. Is not same man who tries ze lederhosen on, your husband. And ve know ziss. Ve cannot do ziss.'

'Pretend you do not know. Please, I beg you. If I do not buy lederhosen now, I will never buy lederhosen.'

The old man pursed his lips. He thought for a few seconds, then turned to the other old man and spoke a stream of German. They argued back and forth. Then, finally, the large man turned back to Mother and said, 'Very well, Madame. As exception —very exception—ve vill know nossink of ziss matter. Not so many come from Yapan to buy lederhosen. Please find man very like your husband. My brother he says ziss.'

'Thank you,' she said. Then she managed to thank the other brother in German. *'Das ist so nett von Ihnen.'*

She—the daughter who was telling me this story—folds her hands on the table and sighs. I drink the last of my coffee, long since cold. The rain is still coming down. There is still no sign of my wife.

'So then?' I say eager to hear the conclusion. 'Did your mother end up finding someone with the same build as your father?'

'Yes,' she replies utterly without expression. 'Mother sat on a bench looking for someone who matched Father's size. Eventually a man came by who fitted the part. Without asking his permission—it seems the man couldn't speak a word of English—she dragged him to the lederhosen shop.'

'The hands-on approach.'

'I don't know. At home Mother was always very sensible,' she says and sighs again. 'The shopkeepers explained the situation to the man, and the man gladly consented to stand in for Father. He put the lederhosen on, and they're pulling here and tucking there, the three of them chortling away in German. In thirty minutes the job was done, during which time Mother made up her mind to divorce Father.'

'Wait,' I say, 'I don't get it. Did something happen during those thirty minutes?'

'Nothing at all. Only those three German men ha-ha-ha-ing like bellows.'

'So what made your mother do it?'

'That's something even Mother herself has never understood. All she knew was, looking at that man in the lederhosen, she felt an unbearable disgust rising in her. Directed towards Father. Mother's lederhosen man, apart from the colour of his skin, was exactly like Father: the shape of the legs, the belly, the thinning hair—and the way he was so happy trying on those new lederhosen, prancing, cocky like a little boy. As Mother stood there looking at this man, so many things she'd been uncertain about her slowly shifted together into something very clear. She realized she hated Father.'

Just then my wife returns from shopping, but while the two of them talk, I'm still thinking about the lederhosen. The three of us have an early dinner, a few drinks, and I keep turning the story over in my mind.

'So, you don't hate your mother any more?' I ask when my wife leaves the room.

'No, not really. We're not close at all, but I don't hold anything against her.'

'Because she told you about the lederhosen?'

'I think so. After she explained things to me, I couldn't go on hating her. I can't say why it makes any difference, I certainly don't know how to explain it, but it may have something to do with us being women.'

'Still, if you leave the lederhosen out of it, supposing it was just the story of a woman taking a trip and finding herself, would you have been able to forgive her?'

'Of course not,' she says without hesitation. 'The whole point is the lederhosen, right?'

Proxy lederhosen, I'm thinking, that her father never even received.

Translated from the Japanese by Alfred Birnbaum

GRANTA

MARTHA GELLHORN
OHNE MICH: WHY I SHALL NEVER
RETURN TO GERMANY

I have been totting up the times that I swore never to return to Germany.

The first was in the summer of 1936 when I saw only a bit of the surface scum, but it was enough. A bunch of youngish beer bellies in brown shirts surrounded an old man and woman, poor people from my quick glance at them, who were on their hands and knees. I thought, but could not believe, that they were scrubbing the pavement. Whatever they were doing was hard and wrong, and these louts were jeering at them.

I was using the *Weltkriegsbibliothek* in Stuttgart for research. The librarian, a thin grey-faced woman, spoke in whispers, saying that they had a new director; she did not know how long the library would stay open. The library documented the Great War of 1914–18, hardly a popular subject, a record of defeat. One afternoon the new director arrived on horseback. He was young, blond and handsome in his brownshirt uniform. He galloped through the trees and untended high grass, and swung from his horse into an open French window. The building was an elegant old house in its own small park. He made a lot of noise in that silent place. The librarian listened with a strange expression; I was unused to the look of fear. Then he rode off, laughing. Though he had gone, the librarian would not answer questions about him or the former director.

I read the newspapers, coarse and belligerent in tone, which is how I learned of the war in Spain, described as the revolt of a rabble of 'Red Swine Dogs'. Those few weeks turned me into a devout anti-fascist. I had not grasped a tenth of the ugliness that pervaded Germany but decided, from disgust, that the country was now worthless. I was never coming back.

But I did, trailing after the soldiery across the bridge at Remagen in March 1945. From then until the end of the war in Europe I saw a lot of Germany. My private war aim was the liberation of the concentration camp at Dachau, the first Hitler had built in 1933. Dachau was a permanent atrocity, far worse than anything I had seen in war. A prisoner skeleton shuffled in to the infirmary where I was listening to Polish doctor prisoners

Opposite: Dresden, 1945.

Photo: Hulton Deutsch Collection

German civilians viewing Auschwitz under Allied supervision.

and announced the German surrender. The same day, in a fever of horror and loathing, I fled Dachau and cadged a lift on a plane ferrying American prisoners of war out of the accursed land. In our different ways, we all swore never to set foot again on German soil; nor were we apt to forget and forgive.

I HAVE NOT talked about how it was the day the American Army arrived, though the prisoners told me. In their joy to be free, and longing to see their friends who had come at last, many prisoners rushed to the fence and died electrocuted. There were those who died cheering, because that effort of happiness was more than their bodies could endure. There were those who died because now they had food, and they ate before they could be stopped, and it killed them. I do not know words to describe the men who have survived this horror for years, three year, five years, ten years, and whose minds are as clear and unafraid as the day they entered.

. . . Dachau seemed to me the most suitable place in Europe to hear the news of victory. For surely this war was made to abolish Dachau, and all the other places like Dachau, and everything that Dachau stood for, and to abolish it forever.

Martha Gellhorn, 'Dachau', May 1945
from *The Face of War*

Then, in September 1946, after the Nuremberg War Crimes Trial had been going on for ten months, I finally felt some sort of duty to witness and report on it. Every day in that courtroom was a soul-sickening history lesson. No one alone could have known the whole story of Hitler's reign. The detail and the scale as pieced together from innumerable witnesses and innumerable documents truly disturbed the balance of one's mind. Meantime the citizens of Nuremberg, looking remarkably fit, kept saying that the concentration camp photographs, plastered over the town for their education, were Russian propaganda, probably pictures of German prisoners of war. And furthermore since we won the war, we could do anything we wanted, so why not shoot Goering and the other Nazi leaders instead of going on with this boring trial. Besides Jews were coming back and actually claiming their old homes and putting German families into the street and, of course, operating the black market. I thought this place and these people were poisonous; the air could not be breathed. Let the Germans rot in their rotten country; nothing would ever bring me here again.

A ROW OF German women sat outside the white tape which marked off the military zone. They were watching their houses. No roof or window remains and often there is not a wall left either and almost everything in those houses has been blown about thoroughly by high explosives, but there they sat and kept mournful guard on their possessions. When asked why they did this, they started to weep. We have all seen such beastly and fantastic suffering accepted in silence that we do not react very well to weeping. And we certainly do not react well to people weeping over furniture. I remember Oradour in France, where the Germans locked every man, woman and child of the village into the church and set the church afire, and after the people were burned, they burned the village. This is an extremely drastic way to destroy property, and it is only one of many such instances. The Germans themselves have taught all the people of Europe not to waste time weeping over anything easy like furniture.

Martha Gellhorn, 'Das Deutsche Volk', April 1945
from *The Face of War*

Sixteen years passed. West Germany was now the favourite ally of the United States government and always referred to as 'the new Germany'. I became curious about the new Germans, those who were innocent of any involvement in the war, so in November and December 1962 I made a long tour of German universities from Hamburg to Munich, listening to students and sitting in on university seminars. With very few exceptions, the young Germans struck me as dismal. Their education was totally dismal. They were taught to learn by heart, to obey not think, and they had learned their lessons well: democracy and anti-communism, which went together, were good; it was necessary to please the great United States, Germany's powerful sponsor. Everyone must work hard and make money for themselves and the prosperity of the state. They were defensive about their parents (none of whom had been Nazis) and humourless; dutiful children reciting the approved ideas. They weren't going to threaten the world, but, dear God, you could perish of boredom here. I escape from boredom wherever I find it; I need never come back to this chastened, respectable, supremely dull country.

IN MY OPINION there is no New Germany, only another Germany. Germany needs a revolution which it has not had and shows no signs of having; not a bloody, old-fashioned revolution, with firing squads and prisons, ending in one more dictatorship, but an interior revolution of the mind, the conscience. Obedience is a German sin. Possibly the greatest German sin. Cruelty and bullying are the reverse side of this disciplined obedience. And Germans have been taught obedience systematically, as if it were the highest virtue, for as long as they have been taught anything . . . . Twice their victors have imposed 'democracy' on a people who never fought for it themselves. Democracy may not be the most perfect form of government, but it is the best we have yet found, because it implies that the citizen has private duties of conscience, judgement and action. The citizen who says Yes to the state, no matter what, is a traitor to his country; but citizens have to learn how to say No and why to say No. Germans are still trained as before in their old authoritarian way; the young are not rebels either. At their best they are deeply troubled by their state and suspicious of it; at their worst they are indistinguishable from their ancestors—the interests of the state come first—and they are potentially dangerous sheep.

Martha Gellhorn, 'Is There a New Germany?', February 1964
from *The View from the Ground*

Nothing would have brought me back except that I worried about the European Community whose full flowering I will surely not live to see but I invest my faith in it. Germany, already the richest European country and, now, reunited, the strongest, began to alarm me: not that I imagined Germany again setting out to conquer Europe by force of arms but that I think Germans collectively are unsound. I think they have a gene loose, though I don't know what the gene is. The present generation of university students, forty-five years after the war, must be truly new Germans and I wanted to look at them, for they would be the future leaders of their own country and possibly of Europe. In November and December 1990, just over a year after the Wall came down, I repeated my 1962 method of touring universities.

They were certainly the best lot of Germans I have ever met. Their education had completely changed and now they were cajoled to think for themselves and speak their own ideas. Young women, for the first time in my experience, were naturally and unaffectedly equal, ready with their opinions. The atmosphere among them was friendly and informal, which was new. The students in East Germany were thrilled that they would be able to travel freely at last, but neither they nor the West German students were excited about reunited Germany. No *Deutschland über Alles* mentality except for a few freaks, regarded as freaks, in Heidelberg. It was odd that none of the young West Germans had foreign friends, though there were foreigners in all their universities; nor did the foreign students I spoke to seem charmed by Germans or eager to know them. The young West Germans assured me that only skinheads and such minor riff-raff were racist about the Turks, and that only nasty housewives took against 'the dirty Poles' who arrived in Berlin in rickety cars, made a lot of noise and litter and bought out the supermarkets, taking the food back for sale in Poland. There is no anti-Semitism in Germany, they said, because they did not feel that hating emotion. I missed irony, of which there were only rare sparks, but that's a fact of German life They're good, decent kids, I concluded with relief; they will make good Europeans.

And then, from this summer onwards, the same kind of

young thugs who were Hitler's Brownshirts began to spring from the paving stones and attacked, in the accepted style, the helpless and weak: refugees. Not Turkish men, who are tough and know how to defend themselves. The German government sat on its hands, while parades, rallies, stonings, hostel burnings proceeded in East Germany. I suspect that this revolting variation on the old Nazi themes may have suited the government as an excuse to change Germany's immigration laws. Those laws were formulated as penance for Germany's Nazi past: having uprooted and destroyed millions, this open-arms policy was a form of apology.

The slowness of the German government to take punitive action and the months of delay before mass public protests are a German problem. But where were the students, where were those good kids? Why weren't their universities alive and fierce with outrage rallies, why weren't they converging on Bonn to demand an end to Hitlerian terrorizing of non-Aryans? Hope deferred maketh the heart sick, as we know. I shall now definitely never go back to Germany, due to hope deferred.

A Turk drove my taxi to the Berlin airport. He was the only Turk I met, though they are so much spoken of. He was very big with a rough voice and threatening moustache. He had been driving a taxi in West Berlin for thirteen years. I asked why he didn't take out German citizenship, wouldn't that make life easier? He said, 'I do not wish to be German.'

GRANTA

Nuha Al-Radi
Baghdad Diary

L ast week I went to the Rashid Hotel to pick up a letter which Bob Simpson had brought from Cyprus. He also sent me some packets of seeds for Italian vegetables, a tiny leak in the embargo: useful, if we ever get any water. His room was full of hacks waiting for the big moment. I told him very authoritatively that there would be no war. He said he wished he could believe me. I'm not sure why I was so positive. I should have known better; after all, I witnessed three revolutions in Iraq, the Suez War in Egypt and most of the Lebanese civil war.

DAY ONE. I woke up at three a.m. to exploding bombs and Salvador Dali, my dog, frantically chasing around the house, barking furiously. I went out on the balcony. Salvador was already there, staring up at a sky lit by the most extraordinary firework display. The noise was beyond description. I couldn't get an answer from Ma and Needles's phone so tried Suha who answered in a hushed voice and said, Put out your lights. Suha was sitting in a shelter she had prepared under the stairs, already stashed with provisions. She'd taped up her windows and doors against nuclear fall-out.

I ventured outside with Salvador to put out the garage light—we were both very nervous. Almost immediately we lost all electricity, so I need not have bothered. The phones also went dead. We are done for, I think: a modern nation cannot fight without electricity and communications. Thank heavens for our ration of Pakistani matches.

With the first bomb, Ma and Needles's windows shattered, those facing the river, and one of poor Bingo's pups was killed in the garden by flying glass—our first war casualty.

DAY TWO. Amal and Munir also lost their windows, so they've moved in here. Ma and Suha will stay here at night. Needles prefers to stay with Menth. M.A.W. only joins us for dinner. Said came by and picked us up to have lunch with Taha—kebabs and beer, delicious. Said has a good supply of petrol (which he's not prepared to share). There were no air raids, and everything seemed normal. Today, all over Baghdad, bread was thrown from government trucks to thronging crowds.

211

DAY THREE. Suha and I spent the day merrily painting while the war was going on full blast outside. I wonder how we manage to feel so detached. This afternoon we saw a SAM missile explode in the sky. I caught Mundher Baig on his grandson's tricycle, his legs scrunched up under his chin, pedalling round and round his garage. He is convinced he will not see his grandchildren again.

At night there was a fire in the orchard, which I thought was from a bomb but in fact had been started by Flayih. He had been burning some dry wood near the dead core of a palm tree, trying to produce coal. It took the whole water supply from Dood's house and mine, plus the fire extinguisher from the car, to put out the fire. Now we have no water. Flayih still has no coal.

DAY FOUR. I woke to an air raid at five and went round to Zaid's house. He was there with his two aunts, both about 110 years old. One was bent double over the stove; the other never stopped chattering. Because of the constant air raids they are afraid to go upstairs to their bedrooms so they sleep in their clothes in the sitting-room. They seem oblivious to the enormity of what's happening around them and concentrate only on the immediate things; that's why, though they are so old and frail, they're so alive and entertaining. Zaid's phone still works so I tried to call Asia and Suha: no answer. Their house is on the river, directly opposite Dora refinery. There is a huge black cloud hanging over that part of Baghdad.

Mundher Baig has made a generator for his house using precious petrol. Ten of us stood gaping in wonder at this machine and the noise it made. Only four days have passed since the start of the war but already any mechanical thing seems totally alien.

Suha is experimenting with a recipe for basturma. The meat in our freezers is thawing so it's a good thing the weather is cold.

In the evening, we cook potatoes in the fireplace. M.A.W. says you can almost taste the potato through the charcoal; admittedly they are burnt. I make a dynamite punch with Aquavit, vodka and fresh orange juice.

DAY FIVE. Munir gave me a calendar today; it's the twenty-first of January. My painting of Mundher Baig and family is nearly finished. I got my bicycle fixed. Although it's new we've been unable to inflate the tyres for days. They both turn out to have punctures. I told the guy mending it that it was new, and he said they always come like this. He thought someone punctures them before they leave the factory. The bike is called Baghdad. At least it's not called Ishtar; the name of our goddess of war that already honours fridges, freezers, soap, matches, heaters and hotels.

We are all now going to the loo in the orchard, fertilizing it and saving water. Janette, who now comes by every day, says that everyone else has gone off to the countryside because it's the best place to be during a war. Then she added that our house is like being in the country anyway. She is looking for someone to share her bed today, quite crazed; I said it wasn't uppermost in my mind right now.

Apparently people take off for the countryside with their freezers loaded on their pick-up trucks and barbecue the food as it defrosts. Only Iraqis would escape from a war carrying freezers full of goodies. We've always been hoarders. Now we have to eat our hoard.

Basil is cooking up all the food from his freezer and feeding it to his cats.

DAY SIX. Got up for the regular five o'clock air raid, which finished an hour later. We went to queue for our petrol ration—twenty litres. Amal, who never remembers to wear her glasses, backed into a wall. The entire country has collapsed and disintegrated in a few days. They say that outside Baghdad everything goes on as normal. I wonder how long we can survive this kind of bombardment. Perhaps we will get water tomorrow.

DAY SEVEN. The worst has happened: we have to drink warm beer. I cleaned out the freezer and removed a ton of different kinds of bread. All I ever had in my freezer was bread, ice and bones for Salvador. Asam had so much chicken in hers that she gave away some and grilled the rest; now Nofa goes around chewing on chicken rather than her usual chocolate bars. She is saving those for harder times, she says. We have to eat everything that will spoil. This means we all shit so much more, all in the garden. If we use the bathroom they say the sewage will back up on us—I have only now discovered an electric pump takes it to the sewage plant. One takes so much for granted. I wonder whether the Allies thought of these things when they planned the bombing. I fear it will be a long time until we have electricity.

Ma began making her own basturma following Suha's recipe. She stuffed the meat and spices into nylon stockings—there are no animal intestines to hand—and hung them in Dood's empty house, in posh marble surrounds. We started burning the rubbish today, clearing the orchard of dead matter. Amal insisted on wearing her high heels, even for collecting brambles.

Rumour had it that there was a difficult night ahead, the seventh, but it clouded over, so maybe God was on our side. I like the idea that some of our Scuds are decoys, probably crafty Russian training. I'd rather we didn't hit civilians but I suppose accuracy is asking too much.

We got some water today, although there wasn't enough pressure to push it up to the roof tank. Still I'm not complaining.

I finished Mundher's painting and we had a little party to celebrate its unveiling. We opened a bottle of champagne and ate *meloukhia* and a million other things. I wish that our stock of food would finish so we could eat a little less. M.A.W.'s sister and brother-in-law fled their house in Fahama and have come to live with him: two more for dinner. His sister left dressed in a green suit, which is all she has now. She is sweet, but hardly says a word; the brother never stops talking and is deaf as a post. He is probably the last surviving communist in the country. In his youth he was well-known for singing old Iraqi songs. He lulled us to sleep with his pleasant voice—dozing heads lolling in different directions.

DAY EIGHT. Silence. It's six in the morning and there's no air raid. I ate so much last night that I couldn't sleep. Depression has hit me with the realization that the whole world hates us. It is not a comforting thought. We have bitten off more than we can chew. Ma's theory is that the world now is ruled by the two smallest powers: Kuwait with its money and oil, and Israel with its power and intellect. It's an unfair world. Other countries do wrong: look what Russia did in Afghanistan, or Turkey invading Cyprus, or Israel taking over Palestine and Lebanon. Nobody bombed them senseless. They were not even punished. Perhaps we have too much history. At least Baghdad is now on the map: I will no longer have to explain where I come from.

I had a recurrent dream before the start of the war: Americans in battle fatigues jogging down Haifa Street, lining up in the alley, kissing each other. They were led by a girl dressed in red. Then suddenly I was on my own and everything was dry as dust, and all I could see was bare earth. What bothered me was the loneliness of the dream. Am I going to be the only survivor?

DAY NINE. Since the war began I have been unable to read a word, not even a thriller. Ma, who usually never stops knitting, can't knit; while Suha and Amal, who have no talent for knitting, have now started. Fastidious Asam, who normally changes her clothes twice a day, now sleeps in the same clothes for two days running. She has hidden all the scissors in her house in case someone breaks in and attacks her with them. She has also wrapped her jewellery in plastic bags, boxed them, and buried them in the garden—hoping that she will remember the exact spot.

I'm trying to get M.A.W. to use his time constructively. I gave him my wall clock to repair. He complained endlessly, then started to fiddle with it and got it to work. He's excellent at mending things, having an endless supply of patience for machines but almost none for life and people. He says if we defeat Israel he'll eat a spoonful of shit—sometimes it's a plateful depending on how good or bad the news. Today he says if we retain Kuwait he'll eat ten platefuls.

Basil came by and I told him to put his mind to basic agriculture. Now that we are back in the Dark Ages we have to figure out a way to haul water up from the river. People have taken to doing their washing in the Tigris, but the river is fast flowing and dangerous. The water situation is bad.

They captured an island in the Gulf that appeared suddenly at low tide: we did not even know its name.

DAY TEN. 'Read my Lips', today is the tenth day of the war and we are still here. Where is your three-to-ten-days-swift-and-clean kill? Mind you, we are ruined. I don't think I could set foot in the West again. Maybe I'll go to India: they have a high tolerance level and will not shun us Iraqis.

Suha mended her bike today. Hers was also new and its tyres were also punctured. We rode out together and caused a sensation in the streets. All very friendly. One guy on a bike sidled by and said he had a Mercedes at home. 'Are we in Paris?' said another. One sour man shouted: 'We don't like girls that ride bikes,' and we yelled at him, 'More fool you,' and rode away. Nofa says I look like ET because I'm wrapped in a hundred scarves and they fly behind me; more like a witch, I'd say. Tomorrow I'll be fifty years old. I feel very depressed. Who the hell ever wanted Kuwait anyway?

M.A.W. says we can get electricity in one minute if we attach ourselves to Turkey or Jordan, because we have a connected circuit. Yesterday we heard we may be getting it from Iran. But what can they connect it to if they bombed the stations?

Everyone talks endlessly about food. While eating lunch the conversation is about what we are having for dinner. We have cooked up all the meat we had. The basturmas we hung in Dood's house are beginning to stink—the whole house reeks.

Hala says she will give me a bucket of water as my birthday present.

DAY ELEVEN. I had great hopes for my birthday. Lots of people were invited, and they all came and more. Drinks flowed in buckets. Someone peed on my bathroom floor (I'm sure it was that horrid Mazin who came uninvited). Fuzzle stayed the night. She said to Yasoub, 'Take me out to pee,' and they went out into the garden arm in arm, so romantic after all these years of marriage. There was a lovely full moon. Fuzzle later entertained us with stories about her air-raid shelter. She goes there every night with Mary, her Indian maid, from six in the evening till seven the next morning. There are three tiers of bunks; the lower one is the most coveted. Fuzzle gets very nervous when the bombing starts, and being diabetic her blood count shoots up. It

Photo: Leonard Freed (Magnum)

was a particularly bad night and we had to take her mind off the noisy bombing outside—she was used to the quiet of the shelter and the soldiers singing to Mary. We must all have the hides of rhinos here in this house; no one seems afraid.

DAY TWELVE. We got water from the taps today. Drew endless buckets up to the tank on the roof. I filled them up below and Munir pulled them up with a rope, eighty buckets in all. Very hard work, and I got soaked in the process.

DAY THIRTEEN. I'm typing by candlelight and can see very little: maybe this won't be legible tomorrow. Ma and Suha went to the souk today to buy more lanterns, and an air raid started. No one bothered to shelter or go home, but just went on with their usual business. In fact there was such a crush that Ma and Suha managed to lose each other. They were bombing the bridge at Southgate. The shock caused all the doors of the buildings in the vicinity to blow open, and all the windows went—broken glass everywhere. Amal's shop, which is right beside the bridge, also got blown up. So now both her house and shop are destroyed. She never complains.

It was Suhub's birthday so we all met there for lunch. Driving across the Adhamiya bridge we could see black columns of smoke rising in all directions. They are burning tyres to confuse the enemy. Some confusion. Samih said that an unexploded rocket had fallen in the garden of the Rashid Hotel, and there was a mad scrabble for mementoes before the security forces sealed it off.

Are we in for a nuclear war? I must say I don't feel there is a risk of death, at least not for myself—I know that I will survive. Twenty-seven thousand bombing raids so far. Is the world mad? Do they not realize what they are doing? I think Bush is a criminal. This country is totally ruined. Who gives the Americans the licence to bomb at will? I can understand Kuwait wanting to destroy us, but not the rest of the world.

The peasant's life that we now lead is very hard, and the work never stops. I get up, come downstairs, collect firewood, clean the grate and make up the evening fire. I clean the kitchen and boil water for coffee. Suha and Amal cook the meals; Ma makes the bread and cakes. I do the soups and salads. I grow all the raw materials for it, lettuce, radishes, celery, parsley and rocca in the orchard. Lunch is a simple snack; dinner—our one meal—is eaten between seven and eight, sometimes accompanied by bombing, other times not.

I have learned to do a lot of things in the dark, except sleep through the night. In fact, we all sleep very little; adrenalin keeps us going.

Salvador has got a new girlfriend. She is horrible. He bit Said yesterday. Salvador is not a dog you can stroke.

DAY FOURTEEN. Mundher Baig died in his sleep. He had a bad heart and yesterday chased up nine floors to check the damage to our building. But he really died of sorrow: he could not comprehend why the world wanted to destroy us. He kept asking Ma yesterday why they were doing it. Somehow I knew while painting his portrait that it would never hang in his house. That was why I finished it in such a hurry, unveiling it before the paint was dry. He was not made for death, so lively and full of energy, good for laughter and for fights. We are going to miss him.

We each chose a section of Baghdad and drove around to inform friends and relatives of the funeral. I went to Mansur, crossing the Adhamiya Bridge during a full-scale air raid. Sirens were going off, rockets and bombs were falling, I was unmoved. Lubna says she saw a plane come down in Karrada; it turned out to be a cruise missile.

DAY FIFTEEN. All the water that Munir and I hauled up to the roof-tank yesterday disappeared through a leak in the downstairs toilet. A tragedy. I have lived in this house for three years and have had to change that loo twice already. It must be jinxed.

I went to help Amal clean up her shop, a mess of broken glass. The holes in Jumhuriya Bridge were neat and precise, with a lot of metal hanging underneath. The bridge was packed with people looking down through the holes. A siren was sounding but nobody moved.

DAY SIXTEEN. The women gathered in Asam's house to pay their respects to Mundher Baig. Word has got round Baghdad that he has died, and people are coming from all over, using up their hoarded petrol. He had apparently been going around Baghdad by bus, checking up on old friends and saying goodbye to them. He must have sensed his coming death.

We may be getting electricity from Qasr Shireen in Iran, but it's all rumours. Nobody knows anything. Baghdad Radio broadcasts for a few hours a day, giving us news of the battle—how many planes we have downed, how we are fighting back—propaganda to keep our spirits up. We listen to Radio Monte Carlo at eight, at night there's the BBC or VOA. Radio Austria is quite sympathetic and actually remembers that there are people living here.

The BBC says our one day battle to take over the tiny island of Kimche was insignificant. But I thought that the Allies came into the war to protect the Saudis, where were they? I think the real issue of this war is the West's inability to accept a strong Arab nation, and a maverick one at that. Iraq is not a servile nation.

Salvador's new girlfriend crawls in through holes in the orchard fence. I keep plugging them but she finds a way in. I had to get up and shoo her away at five this morning—they were making such a racket. Howling dogs combined with the barrage in the sky was too much. The only good thing is that she exhausts Salvador enough to enable us to go to the loo in peace. Otherwise he attacks and terrorizes anyone squatting behind a tree. Amal has it the worst: he grabs at her trousers and tries to pull them off. He thinks it a wonderful game. Now she has to give him a bone every time she goes out, to distract him.

DAY SEVENTEEN. An awful night. Non-stop rockets and the biggest explosion ever. It was heard all over Baghdad but no one seems to know where the bomb landed. It wasn't nuclear anyway, we're still alive. I can understand the Kuwaitis hating us but what did we do to you, George Bush? I can hear it in your voice. Is it because we stood up to the United States?

Tonight we shall have music—Amal has an old crank-up

Victrola gramophone and M.A.W., who never throws anything away, has a lot of 78s. That we should come to this when the rest of the world has CDs.

Widad came today and showed us how to make a candle using a bottle filled with kerosene. You seal the bottle neck with a mash of dates leaving only a small section of the wick sticking out because a long wick produces columns of smoke. An advance: our normal candles leave much to be desired; they splutter, drip, grow enormous wicks and give off black smoke. This bottle-candle lasts for ages. Same principle as a Molotov cocktail except that they are filled with petrol.

This morning there was a huge number of dead flies on the floor. I wonder if the big explosion shocked them to death?

I had a great fight with Salvador, who was cavorting with his white fluffy floozy in one of my flower-beds. They have an entire orchard to gad about—why terrorize my flowers? I don't know what all these lady dogs see in Salvador.

We are a multitude of women in the Suleikh, hardly any men. Now M.A.W. says he wants to leave too. He was touched when we asked him not to.

DAY EIGHTEEN. Last night M.A.W. said, 'We must have continuous war. I have now got so used to eating charred food that when we finish this war we must start another.' We are saving gas by cooking food in the fireplace and baking our own bread on top of an Aladdin stove. These kerosene stoves have proven their worth.

Every night I have surreal dreams. Last night it was people standing outside a third-floor window, having a conversation: a mid-air cocktail party.

The birds have had the worst beating: their sensitive souls cannot take all this hideous noise. All the caged love-birds have died from the shock of the blasts. Birds in the wild fly upside down and do crazy somersaults. Hundreds, if not thousands, have died in the orchard. Lonely survivors fly about in a distracted fashion.

The sky is now covered with black clouds. We are still trying to confuse the enemy by burning tyres. Meanwhile they use computer technology to destroy us. An astronaut on a Russian satellite said he saw huge black clouds and many fires burning across our region.

Salvador has become more used to the noise of the explosions, but an unusually loud bang still sends him chasing about distractedly. The dogs can sense an air raid before it begins; they tense up and start barking. Stray dogs in the orchard pile up against Salvador for comfort during bad air raids. He has us for his security, they have him. Some of them actually cry with fear—the most awful, pathetic sound.

It is a week since we had water. My hands and nails are disgusting. Everyone has a sooty face, and no one looks in the mirror any more. Needles is the only one who still looks neat and clean. Raad says that in Jadiriyah they have no daylight, that the sky is permanently black from the smoke of the Dora refinery as it burns. It has been burning since the first day of the war. Poor Suha and Asia T. How are they surviving?

DAY NINETEEN. Two rockets fell in the Masbah. One on Salwan and Un's garden, crashing into their garage. They were all in the sitting-room—they're OK, if somewhat shaken.

There is nothing nice about war. The one thing that no one envisaged was that Baghdad was going to be bombed like this. They were supposed to be freeing Kuwait. It seems as if the whole conflict was engineered to provide an excuse to destroy our country and our army. No one will hear from us for years. Mundher Baig dead, I can't believe it.

Lubna came by today. Thieves stole his generator and the petrol Mahmoud buried in their garden. Robbery is the fashion. Generators and bicycles go for thousands. Kerosene lamps are valued like gold.

DAY TWENTY. It has now been three weeks. Forty-four thousand air raids. I have another leak in the water system. I will have to check the whole house. Bush says, we make war for peace. Such nonsense. What kind of peace is this? What kind of new world order?

DAY TWENTY-ONE. A week since Mundher Baig died. My hands are now so calloused they look like farmer's hands. Ma says she feels like Scarlett O'Hara in *Gone with the Wind*—though we are far from starving.

They have started targeting bridges again. Jumhuriya Bridge is in three pieces. Textile factories, flour mills and cement plants are also being hit. What do they mean when they say they are only hitting military targets? And as for 'our aim is always true'. Who will save us from these bullies? Maybe they want to destroy us so they can produce more jobs for their people in the West? Reconstruction and new military supplies will keep their economy going for years.

Thamir's hens have stopped laying eggs. They used to produce twenty-five per day, then two and now none. On the other hand, Pat's hens have never laid so many.

Last night I dreamed I was carrying a tree. Little bread rolls grew on it which I was offering around. It had no roots and I was happily walking around with it. Nice. A miracle tree?

DAY TWENTY-TWO. There is a sameness about the days now. I saw the Jumhuriya Bridge today; it's incredibly sad to see a bombed bridge—a murderous action, for it destroys a link. The sight affects everyone that sees it; many people cry.

Children play on streets without traffic. They have never had it so good. They call me Bicycletta and ask me how I am when I pass by. I say fine, or not, depending on my mood. We all know our neighbours; the Suleikh is like one big village. In fact, Baghdad has turned into many little villages.

DAY TWENTY-THREE. The equivalent of five Hiroshimas has already been dropped on us. We could not sleep last night because there were no air raids; we were restless. At midnight the sirens sounded and everyone promptly dropped off.

DAYS TWENTY-FOUR AND TWENTY-FIVE. A sameness. Even war becomes routine.

DAY TWENTY-SIX. It's Monday morning, says the Voice of

America. What's the difference? We had the worst night yet. The minute the all-clear sounded we went to check up on friends and relatives. Everyone piled into Yahya's car. He generously sacrificed the petrol he had been saving (his fiancée lives at the other end of town). We checked on Asam first, then passed by Ma and Needles's house. It was so dark even the river looked black. We couldn't wake up Mohammed, who would sleep through anything, but found Adiba crying and screaming hysterically and repeating over and over again, 'Please God either take my life or that of the bridge.' Her house is very close to the Adhamiya Bridge which they have been trying to knock out for two days now.

Both the Martyrs' and the Suspension Bridges have been hit. I feel very bitter towards the West.

DAY TWENTY-SEVEN. Apparently the awful racket that we heard yesterday was B-52 bombers. They sound horrific.

There are fat cats everywhere. Fat cats sleeping or sitting in doorways, fat cats walking and crossing the streets with no fear of being run over. They of all creatures seem to be totally unmoved by what is happening around them. They have been eating to bursting point all the leftovers from the melting freezers. Thinking of freezers reminds me of Sheikha who returned yesterday to her house, after having spent the last three weeks at her daughter's: her neighbours demanded that she come back because they couldn't stand the smell coming from her house. She put on a face mask and emptied her giant freezer. Right on top, floating on a sea of stagnant scummy water, was an entire sheep; and bobbing around it were twenty-four chickens and sundry legs of lamb in various states of decay; two dozen kubbas; sixty-eight rice patties; plus plastic bags full of stuffed vegetables, beans and peas, three whole fishes, hunks of beef, kilos of minced meat, loaves of bread, cakes and pastries—everything had to be thrown out. Sheika's freezer was like those found in every other well-to-do household in Baghdad. Everyone was preparing and hoarding food in their freezers, never thinking we would lose electricity. The bloated street animals have never had it so good.

I come back from Asam's house to find my home has been invaded by ten more people. They all live near one of the radio stations which today's broadcast says is going to be bombed. I have taken to calling us *Funduq al Saadah*, 'Hotel Paradiso', with every inch of the house now occupied—people playing cards, listening to the radio, boozing. I can't stand it for long.

DAY TWENTY-EIGHT. I am continuously amazed by the solid construction of our houses. Everything shakes and rattles, and yet they stand intact. Last night I felt each and every stone move. The whole of Baghdad shook. They were aiming for the bridge again. No one slept much. We returned to check on Adiba. She is locked inside with her horror of a husband, terrified of him and the bombing—she definitely has the worst of all worlds. Why couldn't he have died instead of Mundher Baig? Not many would have mourned his death.

Why do they keep bombing the same things again and again? Each of these bloody rockets costs a quarter of a million dollars or more. Instead of feeding the hungry of the world, billions are spent on manufacturing more and more sophisticated weapons of destruction. Killing is the new world order.

Muayad and Donny came to visit. The two of them spend their time checking up on the historic buildings around Baghdad, and boarding up their broken windows. A few arches have fallen in Hatra, Ctesiphon has new cracks and the doors of the Mustansiriya exploded open. There is also some damage to the museum from flying shrapnel and debris. Muayad wonders about the state of other sites but does not have the petrol to check them. Where would one start? He is especially worried about the Samarra minaret since the factories and houses nearby (and the people in them) have been virtually flattened. Donny is photographing the damage as evidence. Robbers instantly descend on a building with smashed windows. Muayad and Donny make a wonderful sight—their stomachs arrive in advance of them.

Salvador has a new girlfriend, or rather woman friend (she's no spring chicken). A black and white pup follows her everywhere, no doubt last season's effort. Soon there'll be a whole pile of Salvador pups to add to the pack in the orchard.

DAY TWENTY-NINE. I have moved some of my guests to Dood's house next door. The basturmas, reeking to high heaven, had to be thrown out; we must have done something wrong, perhaps not enough salt. We'll also have to start sharing water with Dood's house, so it's the end of our toilet privileges and a return to the orchard. I cover the previous day's shit with ashes from the fireplace. It is strange but I can't tell the difference between human shit and dog shit.

There are so many people staying here, nineteen between the two houses, that Salvador has forgotten who to bark at. I have been keeping a record of everyone who has been sleeping in the sitting-room, photographing by candlelight. How did painters paint by candlelight? Wonderful shadows—like Caravaggio's or de la Tour's: Ma, Suha and Najul gossiping around a table looking like witches. It's difficult to believe that one day we may have electricity again, turn a switch and have lights on and off at will.

A turning point in the war. They hit a shelter, the one in Ameriya. They thought it was going to be full of a party of bigwigs, not women and children. Whole families were wiped out. The Americans insist that these women and children were put there deliberately. I ask you, is that logical? One can imagine the conversation at Command Headquarters going something like this, 'Well I think the Americans will hit the Ameriya shelter next, let's fill it full of women and children.'

The garden and orchard are beginning to dry out. I use all the washing-up water for the plants. I wish we could have a bit of rain. Tonight was peaceful. Perhaps after Ameriya they will have to be more careful.

DAY THIRTY. A whole month. We are still here, ruined and going strong. Everyone was in the streets firing shots into the air today. What for? Munir said dramatically that it was an invasion. In fact, it was a salute for those who died in the shelter. I think this firing in the air can be interpreted as a sort of protest; in Mosul, they say, there was an actual demonstration.

227

Our big mistake was not to move out of Kuwait by 15 January. That would have left the Allies in a hell of a dilemma. I wish I could see into the future, see what's in store for us.

DAY THIRTY-ONE. We woke up to a totally black sky and the smell of burning gasoline everywhere. A nasty, windy, sandy day. Rain, please come and feed my plants.

I had to go to the doctor—inflamed tonsils, throat and lungs plus a blocked nose. He asked me if I smoked. Very funny. I told him it was from our chimney; at one time it got so bad the room turned black. We couldn't understand what was happening, all of us choking. Munir had a brainwave: perhaps the chimney was blocked. Sure enough it was; shows how poorly our brains are working.

The score today: 76,000 air raids versus sixty-seven Scuds.

DAY THIRTY-TWO. This is the scene in Dood's house: Najul is mother hen and everybody is under her protective wing. When the air-raid siren sounds her grandchildren pile up around her. Everyone else follows behind—daughters, sister, brother-in-law, son-in-law—like a train. Mubajal, who is totally dependent on her sister, insisted on staying close by and spent the first night shivering with fright in the dining-room. A large rat was found lurking in the loo. Mubajal, husband and daughter took their mattresses and went upstairs to a room of their own.

Salvador had a fight with some strays today, and his foot is all swollen. He has now taken to crying when I send his girlfriends away—one white and the other black—I feel terrible.

Ma is making an orange cake in the dark, Suha hovering nearby, learning the recipe. Ma intends to bake it all night long on the dying embers; she hopes it will be like a slow oven.

We stopped burning tyres after the BBC rumbled it; we have invented a new form of camouflage: eucalyptus trees. They are uprooted and made to stand upright between sandbags on bridges. I wonder which genius thought of that.

DAY THIRTY-THREE. I coughed all night. It rained, which was very nice. Between fits of coughing, the air-raid sirens and the bombing I slept about half an hour. Ma's orange cake was burnt on the outside, raw on the inside and tasted of smoke.

DAY THIRTY-FOUR. The streets are black and shiny after the sooty rain; the puddles look like oil slicks. Tariq Aziz has gone to Moscow, but I don't think it will help us. Bush is fighting a dirty war and will hammer us till the bitter end, indifferent to the number of Iraqis he kills. The West has three images of Arabs: terrorists, oil-rich sheikhs and women covered in black from head to toe. I'm not even sure they know that there are ordinary human beings who live here.

Have we hit rock bottom yet?

Hisham came by this morning to offer his condolences for Mundher Baig's death. He was followed by Tim Llewellyn, the BBC correspondent, and the first foreigner I have seen since the war began. When I saw him at the bottom of the drive, I literally bristled. I wonder if he felt it? By the time he had walked up our drive I had overcome my hostility. After all one cannot blame individuals for the actions of governments. Otherwise we would all have to answer for the mess we are in. Tim brought faxes from Sol, Dood and Charlie, our first contact with family and friends—a break in our isolation.

We have a new anti-aircraft gun, a 16mm or whatever, very close by. It makes a beautiful slow dull thud-like noise and adds weight to our nightly open-air concert.

At night, when the sky is covered with great big white and red flashes and our neighbourhood gun is thudding away, it is almost possible to kid oneself that one is attending a Philip Glass opera with an overlay of *son et lumière*.

Mr Bush said no to the overtures of Tariq Aziz—no surprise. It doesn't serve his purpose. He's very brave. He passes judgement on us as he plays golf in Washington.

We had a super barbecue lunch today, a lovely day but quite noisy. I can't bear to hear the Voice of America going on about American children and how they are being affected by this war. Mrs Bush, the so-called humane partner in that marriage, had the gall to comfort a group of American school kids by saying, 'Don't worry, it's far away.'

DAY THIRTY-FIVE. At about ten o'clock this morning Tim returned with a BBC retinue saying that he wanted to do a piece about us surviving *in situ*. I talked, I don't think I was very good. I didn't say any of the things I wanted to say. They filmed us drawing up buckets of water to the roof, and Najul and company camping in Dood's house with Jawdat lying sick on his mattress on the floor. I gave the crew oranges, recently picked from the orchard.

DAY THIRTY-SIX. I just tipped my coffee cup off the stool. I am sitting outside—a delicious day, everything clean and shining after the rains. We had a peaceful night, and the continuing silence seems unnatural.

My first anemones have come out from the seeds I bought last year in the United States. They are white. A sign of peace? Anyway something good from the US of A has grown here.

DAY THIRTY-SEVEN. Pat heard me on the BBC yesterday. I was described as an angry woman. They did not edit out the silly things I had said, like America must be jealous of us because we have culture and they don't, which must be why they have bombed our archaeological sites. But who could envy us?

M.A.W. went to have lunch with Khalil and was given his pet cockerel to eat. It gave him indigestion. Khalil had kept this cockerel for seven years. Recently it had gone crazy and killed two of their hens, before turning on the ducks. Khalil took it to the vet who advised him to cook the cockerel in a *tishreeb*. Imagine cooking a pet you have had for seven years; it's almost cannibalism.

It must have been about nine p.m. and we were all in the kitchen washing up in flickering candlelight. Dinner was a delicious concoction—pasta with a vodka sauce. The pasta was the real thing, inherited from the Italian archaeologists who had rented Dood's house, not stolen Kuwaiti stuff. Suddenly there was a terrible noise and an unreal light, like a sun homing in on us through the kitchen windows. The floor was shaking so violently that we thought the house would come down on our heads. We crouched on the floor and suddenly, without our knowing how, the door had opened and all six of us were outside in the garden. An immense fireball was hovering over us, a fireball that appeared to be burning the tops of the palm trees. Suddenly this giant flaming object tilted and went roaring up into the night sky. Suha was on her knees, arms raised high, screaming, '*Ya ustad*, why here, why in the orchards among the houses?' She calls Our Leader *ustad*, teacher, a polite term considering the world is exploding around us. We later discovered from the BBC that it was a Scud missile, launched from a mobile truck; probably the one that landed in Bahrain. At the time we could not decide whether it was a plane, a missile or a rocket. Or even whether it was coming or going.

Immediately afterwards, while we were still outside, Ma took me aside and whispered hoarsely to me that this was all my fault because I'd said the Americans had no culture. Honestly. Meanwhile, in Dood's house, Najul had thrown herself on top of little Zaynab, and Saysoon had thrown herself on top of them. Then Zaynab's voice was heard saying she wanted to get up, Najul said no, and the answer came back, 'In that case I am going to pee in my pants.' Zaynab's reaction to every air raid is to want to pee.

At four-thirty a.m. Ma came into my bedroom with a candle and said it seems we have agreed to the Moscow initiative. The land attack started at four. At five-thirty we all go down and make coffee.

DAY THIRTY-EIGHT. Everyone is terribly depressed today. Amal walked off without any breakfast when a discussion became too heated. We had to go after her, and she returned tight-lipped and disapproving. I think it is a bit much: surely we are all entitled to say what we like here. If one can't think and talk freely at home then one might as well give up. Needles also showed up with bag and baggage, Menth carrying her bedding behind her and saying we should all feel rotten together. Ma yelled at her too, and they had a fight. Menth said this is why she had come.

It's a balmy day; spring is everywhere. It is difficult to believe that there is a war on even though we have already had two air raids this morning, planes all over the sky. Fuzzle came by and cooked us a delicious hot lentil lunch.

Apparently last night's Scud was seen and heard all over the Suleikh. Everyone thought it was directly above us. It was launched from somewhere near our bridge. How and with what does one ignite (is that the right word) a Scud? How far back does one have to stand? They seem to be horrifically inaccurate and erratic machines.

Other people have heard me on the BBC—it seems the interview has also been broadcast by the Arabic service. Amal is miffed because they did not use what she had said.

Air-raid sirens sound only after the planes have come and gone. White streaks across the sky, the sound of bombs falling and then the siren goes. I don't know why they bother. I'm glad our ineptitude has not been publicized yet.

We had a barbecue dinner through the air raid, but our hearts were not in it.

DAY THIRTY-NINE. Today is as ugly as yesterday was beautiful; the air is thick with smog. God knows what they are burning. It's noon and we have had five raids already. My cough will not go away. How many Hiroshimas so far? Tim Llewellyn says that the Iraqis are resigned to their fate. It's true, we are just waiting now, a few days, a few weeks. Bush and the Emir of Kuwait had a breakfast date in Kuwait on the twenty-fifth. Well, it's the twenty-fifth today and they are not breakfasting together. Small comfort.

DAYS FORTY AND FORTY-ONE. Nights and days full of noise, no sleep possible. For forty days and nights, a Biblical figure, we have stood with our mouths open swallowing bombs. We didn't have anything to do with the Kuwaiti takeover, yet we are paying the price for it. We are living in an Indian movie, or better still we are like Peter Sellars in *The Party*, refusing to die, rising up again and again for a last gasp on the bugle. Indian movies never really end.

Tim came by to pick up the letters. He is leaving to go back to Cyprus. I was pruning the roses and taking cuttings in Najul's house. Gardening is my only relief—nothing beats plants as soothing company. When I feel aggressive I cut and prune; when I feel hopeful I plant.

DAY FORTY-TWO. Defeat is a terrible feeling. This morning, the forty-second day, the war stopped. They kept at us all night long, just in case we had a couple of gasps left in us. It was the worst night of bombing of the whole war. Nobody slept a wink. I think they dropped all the left-over ammunition.

They say the Americans are in Nasiriya. Will they enter Baghdad? As in my dream, will they come marching down Haifa Street?

3 MARCH. The war has been over for some days. Today Schwarzkopf met with whoever we sent as representative. We agreed to everything. After all the hyperbole that they use against us, the Americans are now simply sitting in Nasiriya checking people's ID. Meanwhile our national radio continues to broadcast our victory. We fought thirty-two nations and are still here! True—until one looks at the condition that we are in.

Stories of returning soldiers are endless, even high-ranking officers are walking home from the south, a total breakdown of the system. It apparently takes from a week to ten days to walk the distance from Kuwait to Baghdad, all the time dodging Allied planes; the Jaguars in particular keep trying to pick off the stragglers. Who flies Jaguars other than the Brits? And they call themselves civilized, hitting at retreating and unarmed soldiers. All the wounded who could not run away fast enough were killed. The others walk with no food or water, and collapse in heaps when they arrive at their houses.

7 MARCH. We had such a storm yesterday—wind, black sky, rain, an orange-coloured sand storm, then rain again and howling wind. Two palm trees came down in Needles's orchard; they crashed right on to our fence, bringing it down. Now it's open to the wild dog packs. We have had to kill six dogs so far, and bury them in the orchard.

Sections of Baghdad already have electricity; some say we will get it tomorrow. I don't believe it. It apparently comes for a day and then goes off. I'm sure someone is trundling the same generator around to different parts of Baghdad to give everybody a taste. I have forgotten what it feels like to turn on a light switch. Rumour has it that Basra has fallen again.

8 MARCH. Just returned from a yummy lunch of smoked salmon—Lubna had given me some before the war, and I stored it with Abbas who has a generator. Took it out today and ate it at Dhafir and Mutaza's. They had electricity—and ice! Mutaza says that electricity shows up the dirt in your house, and that ever since hers came on she has been cleaning like a demented woman. I dread to think what my house is going to look like; that soot from the chimney must have left a thick film on everything.

10 MARCH. It is ten-thirty at night and I have five candles burning in my room: what an extravagance. By the time one has filled up the bottle candles with kerosene, cleaned the lamps and the grate, picked up the day's fallen oranges in the orchard, swept and cleaned the house, gathered firewood and thrown a few stones at roaming dogs, the day is over. I sold fifty-two kilos of oranges today for 116½ dinars. There is no petrol, no electricity, no running water and no telephone.

Hala was very funny today, ranting about how she has missed out on life and would die a virgin. She yelled hysterically at her mother, 'At least you have your husband to sleep with.' Nothing but bleakness looms ahead, certainly not a fancy love life. In the street one sees plenty of men but our houses are full of women. There are so few men in our lives.

12 MARCH. Many macabre funny stories. One about a taxi driver coming back from the front with a dead soldier's coffin on top of his car. He was searching for the poor bugger's parents and went into a house to ask the way—only to find his taxi and the coffin gone. There are no police to complain to. Another story is about a government truck selling gas bottles in the street. When the bottles had all been sold and the driver was ready to move off he discovered there was no petrol in the car. It had all been

siphoned off. Sheikha says that the only thing the West knows about us is the fable of 'The Thief of Baghdad'—perhaps they are right.

Tahsin, the grocer, told me that he had heard me talk on the BBC. He asked me what it was like outside, in the UK. I could not think of much to say except that it rains so much there that your bones get wet. He thought for a minute and then said, 'I guess every place has its pros and cons.' A sweet man. His mother Khairiya, a lovely smiley lady, took literacy classes and came top, but now can't read a thing, having forgotten it all. Ma and Needles's maid also had to take those classes but after three years she was still unable to read bus numbers.

Munir crashed into some pole while on his bike and smashed his face and nose.

13 MARCH. We had the black clouds with us again today and it rained. All our houses are streaked with huge black drips, which fall from the parapets of the roofs. It's the new fringed look. I wonder if our lungs have the same patterns.

14 MARCH. What a way to raid a country—apparently we denuded Kuwait of everything plus the kitchen sink. Airplanes, buses, traffic lights, appliances, everything. Our shops are full of their goods. We know nothing about our situation.

We may have petrol by Sunday. Bush says he is worried about the mess that we are in. My, how decent of him. I must do something or go mad—perhaps build a swimming pool?

16 MARCH. Yesterday Suha got electricity. M.A.W. came here and we played cards. He is always complaining that I cheat because I peer into his hands. But he holds out his cards right in front of my face, says he can't see too well by candle and lamplight. Not my fault.

More irises are out. It was deadly quiet during the day because the security forces were out checking for arms in houses in the Grey'at area near us. They searched Khalil and Amal's houses. They took away Khalil's typewriter even though he has permission for it. I wonder if I should hide mine. He was very upset with the officers because they fingered everything, including his wife's underwear. I asked him how he could have eaten his favourite pet cockerel. He said that he was feeling so guilty about the whole episode that he had been having disturbed dreams about it for days.

17 MARCH. The stories are getting more grotesque. Kufa, Kirkuk and Basra, bodies and bodies lie everywhere. In Kufa it seems they (who?) have pillaged the university buildings and burned papers and documents in the library—more devastation and destruction.

18 MARCH. I had an endless stream of visitors today at the studio, Asia and Suha T. included. The bombing had been so bad near them that they spent the entire time on the floor of the laundry room, all piled up together, sharing the space with a large rat who delivered a litter in their midst (she says). It was the only room in the house that did not have outside windows, and they felt safe there. All their windows along the river, across from the Dora refinery, were broken.

19 MARCH. In the coffee shops the talk is not of nationalism, but of the desire for the US to come in and take over—get it over with. Our television coverage remains the same.

20 MARCH. A gang robbed Umberto's house of a thousand crates of beer which he had been storing for his company. Only his clothes and the beer were taken. Each crate of beer sells for eighty dinars. That is 80,000 dinars right there, a fortune. No one steals electrical goods any more. Petrol, beer and cigarettes are the popular items, although oddly they all go for the same price.

It seems we will be allowed to travel from 1 June. Human rights dictate that people can travel and we must follow those guidelines. Human rights?

28 MARCH. It is too depressing to write. I keep saying that it can't get worse and it does.

Met Mohammed G.'s sister today, recently fled from Kerbela. She saw horrific sights, dead bodies left on the street, relatives too frightened to remove them, bodies being eaten by dogs and cats. They have been bulldozing the area around the mosque and shrine; people were given three days to clear out of their houses. All of the old Kerbela will disappear. The whole thing is sick.

I have a new war: against snails. A least ten billion snails have invaded the orchard—that is the round figure that is being bandied around for everything these days; it might as well apply to my snail count. They eat every green thing they see; they even ate my new baby magnolia, transplanted recently from Asam's garden. She says these things happen only in my garden, never hers. The dogs are on the increase again. Poor Salvador, he has to pee so much to mark his territorial boundaries that his leg is permanently poised in mid air. He is quite exhausted and probably dehydrated.

We came back walking tonight, pushing our bikes. Nearly a full moon. Naylah only found out her brother was alive when her husband in London saw him on television , a hostage in Saudi Arabia—live on CNN, as they say.

RAYMOND CARVER   JAYNE ANNE PHILLIPS   JOY
WILLIAMS   T CORAGHESSAN BOYLE   JOHN
UPDIKE   TOBIAS WOLFF   BARRY HANNAH   ANN
BEATTIE   JAMAICA KINCAID   WILLIAM GASS
DAVID LEAVITT   JANE BOWLES   ROBERT PENN
WARREN   JOHN CHEEVER   PAUL   BOWLES
SHIRLEY JACKSON   EUDORA

GRANTA BOOKS

THE
BOOK OF THE
AMERICAN
SHORT STORY

EDITED BY RICHARD FORD

WELTY   HAROLD BRODKY   MALAMUD
FLANNERY O'CONNER   GRACE PALEY   JAMES
BALDWIN   VONNEGUT
JEAN STAFFORD   JOYCE CAROL
OATES   DONALD BARTHELME   JAMES ALAN
MCPHERSON   ROBERT COOVER   LEONARD
MICHAELS   GAYL JONES   WILLIAM KOTZWINKLE
JOHN UPDIKE   HARD YATES
MAX APPLE   RICHARD
BAUSCH   STORE   TIM
O'BRIEN   ANNE
PHILLIPS   RAGHESSAN
BOYLE   JOHN   WOLFF   BARRY
HANNAH   ANN BEATTIE   JAMAICA   KINCAID

'These are wondrous stories . . . They treat us to language. They stir our moral imaginations. They take our minds off our woes, and give order to the previously unordered for the purpose of making beauty and clarity anew. They do the best for us that fiction can do' - **Richard Ford, 1992**

WILLIAM GASS   DAVID LEAVITT   JANE BOWLES
ROBERT PENN WARREN   JOHN CHEEVER   PAUL
BOWLES   SHIRLEY JACKSON   WALLACE STEGNER
EUDORA WELTY   HAROLD BRODKY   BERNARD
MALAMUD   FLANNERY O'CONNER   GRACE PALEY
JAMES   BALDWIN   PETER   TAYLOR   KURT
VONNEGUT   JEAN STAFFORD   STANLEY ELKIN

GRANTA

Notes from Abroad

Zagreb, Autumn 1992
Dubravka Ugrešić

*I*s there life before death? I happened to remember this Romanian riddle from the museum of communist black humour a little while ago, and for the first time it made me think seriously.

'No,' said my mother decisively. 'All there is is survival.'

In Croatia the word *survival* has completely replaced the word *life*. If we can just somehow survive, sighs my neighbour. The main thing is that we're alive, we'll survive somehow, says a friend. In times like these the most important thing is to survive, Mme Micheline concludes positively. Mme Micheline survived the Second World War, the first independent state of Croatia, communist Yugoslavia, the second independent state of Croatia, another war; she knows what she's talking about.

After being out of Zagreb for several months, I am prepared to tackle the business of survival head on.

'The most important thing is not to get upset and not to eat pork,' says my mother.

'Why?' I ask.

'Because people say that butchers have been finding gold chains, rings, tooth crowns, in pig carcasses . . . ' whispers my mother conspiratorially, and then adds calmly: 'I don't eat meat anyway.'

'Why not?'

'Because it's expensive.'

*T*he person who has resolved to survive needs identity papers. After many hours spent queuing for an ID card, I finally reached the counter.

'Nationality?' yelled the clerk.

'Anational,' I replied.

'There's no such thing!' she bellowed.

'Don't you have some heading for . . . "others"?'

'No! Just tell me what you are and stop making a nuisance of yourself!' said the clerk addressing the queue this time, exactly as prescribed in Soviet handbooks of totalitarian etiquette.

'She must be Serbian, and she's afraid to say so,' commented someone behind me.

'Are you Serbian?' asked the clerk.

'I'm anational.' I elaborated: 'Undetermined.'

'How can anyone be "undetermined" in this war?' screamed the clerk.

'I'm not undetermined in the war, just under the heading "nationality".'

'Say you're Croatian and get on with it,' whispered the person behind me benevolently.

'I can't,' I said. 'Not as long as belonging to a particular nationality makes one citizen of this state politically, socially and humanly acceptable, and another unacceptable,' I explained to the benevolent person, pleased that I had been able to formulate my position so satisfactorily.

'Listen, I've a friend, a Serb, who registered as a Gypsy. Say you're a Gypsy, that's OK.' He was determined to help me.

'I am—others!' this time I yelled as well, and for some reason reinforced my position by repeating 'O-T-H-E-R-S!' in English.

'There are people waiting! I'll write "others" for you and you can go to hell!' the clerk spoke to the whole queue again, and I finally got my essential document confirming that I was a citizen of Croatia.

G iven that I am not a refugee and that I still have a job, my chances of survival are greatly enhanced. I budget carefully for bread and milk. I don't pay rent, electricity, heating or telephone bills. I don't buy newspapers, which is no hardship. I don't eat meat. Instead of fruit and vegetables I chew American vitamin pills (I have a year's supply). I've given my clothes to refugees. I hardly need any shoes as I don't go out. Instead of cosmetics I use the remains of the real Dalmatian olive oil I bought last year on the island of Brac. I've learned not to complain. The other day I mentioned to my neighbour that I couldn't buy face cream. Look what we've come to, I said, olive oil . . .

'You should be glad that you're alive, that you've got a roof over your head and that you're not a cripple. Imagine if you had been at the front and now you had to push yourself around in a wheelchair,' said my neighbour sternly.

'Heavens, yes.'

'Or perhaps you would like Milošević to come? said my neighbour in a terrible voice, thrusting her face into mine.

'Goodness no, God forbid,' I said.

'Those dreadful Serbs could be raping and torturing you now in some camp. Is that what you want?' my neighbour got more and more excited.

'That would be terrible,' I said. I could feel myself trembling.

'Or perhaps you'd like us still to be living in the prison of nations?'

'What prison of nations?'

'Why, the former Yugoslavia.'

'Oh no, definitely not in a prison,' I said.

'Well, then, if you think about it, we're really well off!' said my neighbour.

'Absolutely,' I said.

And for some reason I pushed the bottle of olive oil into her hand.

'Take it,' I said, moved.

'Thank you,' she said. 'It'll come in handy for potato salad.'

don't complain about everyday life any more. I'm an expert on Russian literature: I've read Zoshchenko, Il'f and Petrov. I wrote my doctorate on Bulgakov. I know totalitarian mechanisms, at least literary ones, by heart. I just never expected to be living them. Especially not now we have democracy. In the former Yugo-communist regime (I've learned the jargon), queues were definitely shorter and salaries were higher. And there were fewer 'Russian' scenes. But I keep quiet about that. I could be accused of Bolshevism. And we all know who the 'Bolsheviks' are: Serbs, Chetniks, Yugo-aggressors, our deadly enemies who got us into this.

I know and accept that culture is not a priority in wartime —I don't go to the cinema (there could be a bomb) or buy books (there aren't any)—though in wartime everyone likes to talk about writers. For some reason, all post-communist states like to have writers to lead them. Half the Serbian parliament are writers; even our President doesn't hide his love of literature. As soon as a writer dear to the regime dies, the President immediately appears on television to express his condolences.

'We'll print your book if you bring us 140 kilos of paper,' says my friend, a publisher.

'Where can I find 140 kilos of paper?'

'I don't know. That's your problem, you're the writer,' says my friend.

I sometimes think nostalgically of a distant totalitarian year I spent in Moscow. My friends—painters, writers, intellectuals —lived in happy opposition to the regime, underground, up to their eyes in 'samizdat'. What a creative and stimulating life that was! Here, we live on the surface, we voted for a democratic government and—What's got into me? Am I mad? Do I want icing on the cake? I've confused the times: can't I distinguish democracy from totalitarianism any more?

I'll survive, I think to myself. I won't go out. I won't see anyone. I have noticed with satisfaction that a crust of indifference is settling round my heart. I don't get upset. If a Serbian house explodes I repeat the responses I've heard: What do they expect when they built on our land? And I see that everyone around me approves. If an innocent Serb is attacked, I don't protest; I say: Let them see what it's like to be beaten up when you've done nothing. And no one frowns, no one comments, everyone nods in unison. It is as though the whole country, my sweet little Croatia, has turned into a school choir, obediently singing in chorus.

I don't upset myself any more; I've decided to survive. I watch the public lynching of people who have the audacity to think for themselves in this 'most democratic country in the world' (as its President frequently calls it). I see how Croatian television has become an arena for public lynchings. (The Television Director is the President's best friend.) I watch monuments being destroyed everywhere: to Nikola Tesla in Glina, to Ivo Andrić in Visegrad, to the victims of fascism on the island of Brac. I don't upset myself, why should I? Our towns have been razed to the ground, for goodness' sake, and I'm getting agitated about some monuments. Besides, it's natural in a democracy that people put up the monuments they want and scrap the ones they don't care for.

'We've always built—it's in our genes. We may destroy something along the way, but that's a habit we've picked up from those barbarians, the Serbs,' says my neighbour.

'That's right,' I say, remembering my decision to survive.

Sometimes I feel sick when I see the mixture of fear and adoration on the faces of the people, and their shamelessly public longing for an autocratic leader. I feel sick when I hear my fellow-citizens calling their democratically elected President 'father', 'dad' or 'the old man', quite forgetting that 'the old man' was what they called Tito just ten years ago.

I find survival a little harder when I see on television shots in which all the participants point little crosses towards the camera, like actors in vampire movies. Men with open shirts so that the cross can be seen more easily, women with bare necks and *décolletés* . . . The crosses signal frantically to the viewers that we are all true believers, Western, cultured; we are not wild beasts thirsty for blood like our enemies. But I'll cope with that too. I'm not stupid, I know what the priorities are. A little cross here or there is trivial compared to the loss of life. (Though a cross sometimes reminds me of its opposite—the metal identification tags round soldiers' necks which are put in the soldiers' mouths when they're dead.)

An acquaintance of mine developed a serious illness.
I want to survive, he said. I have to live with my illness in order to conquer it. My acquaintance survived, but he changed a lot. He has an absent look, is incapable of being stimulated by the outside world, is forever holding his wrist feeling for his pulse, listening to his own heart beating. Sometimes the shadow of hatred passes over his pale, washed-out face. I hate the healthy, he says simply.

The state of survival is a state of emotional, social and moral autism. People determined to survive are an odd bunch. Perhaps next month instead of bread and milk I'll buy petrol and set fire to myself on the main square in Zagreb like Jan Palach.

'Plagiarism,' an informed passer-by will say. 'Jan Palach set fire to himself as well.'

'True,' someone else will say. 'What did he do that for?'

Translated from the Croatian by Celia Hawkesworth

Dobrinja
Nedžad Ibrišimović

DAY FOURTEEN OF THE SIEGE OF DOBRINJA. Adem Kahriman is writing a book. Adem lives on the fifth floor; I live on the fourth. Our windows share a view of Sarajevo's airport and the Igman hills beyond. The hills change colour constantly, day and night, and are always beautiful. The snowy peaks of the mountain of Treskavica sometimes appear through the mist. Adem likes the snow. He is fifty-two years old. He wants to write a book which will prevent the crimes that have already happened in the past.

What kind of man is Adem Kahriman?

He was born in Sarajevo. But to say that is a little confusing: How can anyone be born in Sarajevo? He is not fair-skinned. But that is not right either. Maybe this would be best: hair greyish, no moustache or beard, features regular, no personal marks.

Plato says that a man is a being with two legs and without feathers. This definition could, with a light conscience, be applied to Adem Kahriman. Adem's being is concentrated in the upper half of his body: in his heart and head. He has a soul, he is sensitive and honest, he has a feeling of presentiment and an ability to understand men before they speak. When Adem is alone, the thought of people horrifies him. All animals are incomprehensible to Adem, but he loves watching them.

Perhaps it is easier to explain what kind of writer Adem Kahriman is: he is good, very good, but unknown.

This is the first sentence of Adem's book: 'In 1942 the Chetniks skinned the back of Haji Tahirović from Foča. They pulled the skin over his head and pinned a note to him which read: "veiled muslim woman".'

How is Adem Kahriman going to prevent the Chetniks from skinning Haji Tahirović when they've already done it?

Adem began his book in April this year. As it happens, during the same month, a man who also writes books, a professor, kicked a human head in the village of Tabaci. Tabaci, coincidentally, is situated in the hills surrounding Foča.

The professor wasn't kicking this head on his own. There was also a Bosnian government minister—someone, in any event, to kick the head *to*. Someone, also, who could kick the head *back*. I assume that they must have washed their shoes afterwards. I wonder if they turned up their trousers.

The human head that the Bosnian minister kicked to the professor and that the professor then kicked back to the minister, was once on the shoulders of a peasant from the village. The peasant had kept a flock of sheep; indeed he was well-known in the area for the quality of his flock. He was not beheaded straight away: first he was asked for ten lambs, and then brandy—a lot of brandy—and then thirty sheep. Everyone sat round the peasant's table on wooden benches—the minister, the professor and seven Chetniks. The peasant refused to hand over his sheep. They asked him for money. Again he refused. So three Chetniks took him to the woods behind his house. That's where they killed him.

There was perhaps another reason: the peasant was not a Serb. The Drina River—near which the peasant lived—was meant only for Serbs. At least this was what the men who write books in Belgrade believed.

DAY FIFTEEN OF THE SIEGE OF DOBRINJA. 'How do you intend to prevent the crimes that have already happened?' I ask Adem Kahriman.

'By the book I started to write,' answers Adem.

'But that's impossible.'

'Have you read the first sentence?'

'Yes, I have.'

'Did you know of the fate of Haji Tahirović from Foča before you read that first sentence?'

'No, I didn't.'

'Well, you know now?'

'I do.'

'And can you see him?'

'I can.'

'Do you see him dead?'

'No. I see him alive in that horrible state.'

'Well,' said Adem, 'the only thing left for me to do is to prevent them from skinning him.'

'But how?'

'It may be impossible but at least I'll try,' Adem Kahriman said.

That same day, Chetniks entered one of the villages above Rogatica and gathered the men together. They were then burned to death.

COMMENTS. *Chetnik*: The word derives from the one used for troop (*ceta*). There are several features characteristic of Chetniks. They tell lies. They are Serbs. They massacre the Bosnians. It is through massacres—or precisely through slaughtering, killing, burning, raping and robbing—that Chetniks hope to conquer the country of Bosnia. The Chetniks are defenders of the Serbian cause. The Serbian cause is all things Serbian: men, women, birds, fish, plants, even the Serbian crow. Note the following concern expressed by Dr Svetislav Zec in his book, *On Serbian Nature* (Zemum, 1938): 'In the last thirty years it has been noticed that the flight of the Serbian crow has become more slothful and if such a tendency continues the Serbian crow will stop flying in less than a hundred years.' It is not any old crow: it's the Serbian crow—a matter of concern.

Sarajevo: The capital of Bosnia, a place of mosques, cathedrals and churches (not to mention singers and actors). The town is surrounded by mountains; through it flows the shallow

Miljacka River, flanked by high white walls and broken intermittently by waterfalls and bridges—each bridge as beautiful as the entrance to a palace. The word *Sarajevo* comes from the Turkish word *saraj* which means palace, and is first mentioned in 1507.

In 1697 Eugen Savojski robbed and burned Sarajevo. In the next 300 years Sarajevo was burned five times more. The town now extends behind the mountain of Trebevic to Dobrinja. That's where Adem Kahriman and I live.

Bosnia: A good country.

Bosnia and Herzegovina: The same, except that the mountains in Herzegovina are bare.

Drina: A beautiful, cold river, which connects and separates the country of Bosnia from the country of Serbia. There are gardens on its banks which illustrate what I believe paradise to be. The hills above are high and gentle; quiet breezes blow down from them.

DAY SIXTEEN OF THE SIEGE OF DOBRINJA. 'Is Haji Tahirovic still in pain?' I ask. I am concerned.

'He is,' Kahriman replies and adds, 'read this.'

In the early morning of the last Thursday of March 1942, the Chetniks entered the village of Vrsinje, a few kilometres away from the place of Milici. They gathered together all the people they found, pushed them into a *masdzid* and burned it. One hundred eighty-three living human beings died that morning in Vrsinje, burned to death. Among these 183 martyrs there was also a local muallim, Husein efendi Talović, and the members of his family: his wife, his four sons and his daughter.

'If you cannot prevent this,' I say, 'then don't show me any more.' The whole idea is that Adem is going to prevent the crimes that have already occurred.

'Rain!' Adem said quietly. 'Heavy rain will put out the fire!

They are saved!'

'Yes, but only in your book.'

'All the same,' Adem says.

Suddenly, Adem pulls me by my sleeve to crouch down on the floor; he squats down himself. We hear shots outside. The shelling has resumed. It is the sixteenth day of shelling Dobrinja from the Lukavica barracks. We crawl out into the corridor. For some reason, we always feel safer in the corridor.

'For the first few days of the shelling,' Adem says, still whispering, 'you couldn't hear sparrows at all—did you notice? They had stopped singing entirely. After the first week, they reappeared and you could hear them between shots. Now you can hear them constantly whether there are shots or not.'

COMMENTS. _Vrsinje_: A village of a few houses, a school, some cottages. The surrounding hills are just like those in Arabia, but they are grassy. To be fair, the hills in Vrsinje are white in winter, and hills in Arabia are not. It never snows in Arabia in winter.

Mesdzid: A mosque without a minaret and various other things which I shouldn't list here because I would then have to explain them. The _mesdzid_ is where the Chetniks burnt 183 people alive. Although all those men, women and children were burnt by the Chetniks and not by the communists, the communists did not allow people from Vrsinje to rebuild their _mesdzid_ for fifty years.

Muallim: Religious teacher.

Partisan: Tito's fighter.

COMMENTS ON THE COMMENTS. _Josip Broz Tito_: He was the supreme commander of partisans who beat Chetniks and Ustashas in 1945. After he died in 1980, his country divided, and Serbo-Chetniks took all the arms of his army. At the beginning of the Second World War, Tito asked the Chetniks twice to join the partisans in their fight against fascists, and they said they would do so but they lied.

A group of partisans, a few Serbs and a Muslim whose name

was Mustafa Dovadžija, stood on the slope of Crepoljsko mountain on a lovely spring morning.

'Dear comrade, come and join us,' Serb partisans said amiably.

Mustafa went with them, suspecting no evil. Shortly afterwards partisans suddenly turned into Chetniks and impaled Mustafa alive. It was on 2 May 1942.

This is how Ivo Andrić, our Nobel Prize winner, described it:

> On the ground was an oak pole, two and a half metres long, with a sharp iron point. When they ordered Mustafa to lie down he lowered his head, then the Chetniks approached him and started stripping off his coat and shirt. Saying nothing, the partisan lay down with his face turned to the ground as he was told. Then they tied each of his legs with a rope. Two Chetniks then pulled his legs wide apart. At the same time, Jovan, another Chetnik, rested the pole against two logs, so that the pole's top was now between the victim's legs. He pulled a short, wide dagger out of his belt, kneeled before the out-stretched man and cut the cloth of his trousers between his legs to widen the opening through which the pole would enter the body. The tied body of the sufferer shuddered from the short stab of the knife, raised its upper part as if trying to get up, but immediately fell down again hitting the ground. The horrifying part of the butcher's work completed, Jovan jumped back, grabbed a wooden mallet and began to hit the lower, dull part of the pole with slow and steady strikes. He stopped and looked down at the body into which he was driving the pole and then at the two Chetniks, reminding them to pull more slowly and evenly. The body of the stretched man clenched at every strike of the mallet, his spine stooped and bent, but the ropes tightened and straightened him again. One could hear how the wretch hit his forehead against the ground,

and also some very peculiar sound. It wasn't a scream or a cry or a death rattle or any kind of human sound. All that stretched and tortured body could produce was a kind of squeaking and banging, as if someone was splicing logs for a fence. After each strike, Jovan now went over to the stretched body, bent over it, checked whether the pole was going in a good direction and, after he made sure that none of the vital parts was injured, resumed his task. For one moment the striking stopped. Jovan had noticed that the muscles at the tip of the right shoulder had tightened and that the skin of the wretched man was lifting. He approached him quickly and cut the bulging spot cross-wise. Pale blood gushed, at first weakly and then more strongly. Two or three slow and careful strikes more and the iron-hemmed tip of the pole began to emerge at the cut spot. He struck several times more, until the tip of the pole was level with the tip of the right ear. The man was impaled as if he was a lamb ready for a barbeque, except that the tip of the pole wasn't coming out of his mouth but out of his back, and that neither his insides nor his heart or lungs were seriously injured. Jovan threw down the mallet and approached the man on the ground. He examined the body, avoiding the blood which was dripping from the place where the pole entered and had formed small pools on the ground. The two Chetniks turned the stiff body on its back and began to tie his ankles to the pole. At the same time Jovan was checking to see that the man was still alive and looking at the face which, all of a sudden, became swollen, bloated and larger. His eyes were wide open and restless, but his eyelids were motionless; his lips had stiffened in a kind of cramp, while his clenched teeth were glimmering behind them. He wasn't able to control some face muscles; his face looked like a mask. His lungs moved in short and rapid breaths. The two Chetniks began lifting him as though he were a piece of meat prepared for cooking. Jovan was shouting at them, warning them to take care, to keep the body steady, and he himself assisted them. They drove the lower, thicker part of the pole into the ground, propping up the back with a short stick, which they nailed to the pole.

The three Chetniks left to join the rest of the group. At that empty place Mustafa Dovadžija remained alone on the pole, one metre from the ground, with his chest thrown out, stripped to his waist. From a distance one could hardly guess that the pole went through his body, with his ankles tied to it and his arms tied at his back.

Chetniks then approached the tortured man, examining him closely. Only a weak stream of blood was running down the pole. He was alive and aware. His sides were rising and falling. The veins on his neck were pulsing. His eyes were rolling slowly but he could see. Through his clenched teeth a kind of drawling growling was pouring out and one could only understand some words in it: 'Chetniks, Chetniks,' he was sobbing, 'I wish you die like dogs . . . Die like dogs!'

It is 11 July 1992, the seventeenth day of the siege of Dobrinja. We saw part of the sky, a part of a hill and a part of the next building. Not far from Dobrinja in the settlement of Hrasnica, Chetniks shelled the kindergarten, killed four and injured ten children.

DAY EIGHTEEN OF THE SIEGE OF DOBRINJA. Adem said: 'First they attack the apartment blocks with tanks, anti-aircraft machine-guns and canons. Then they enter the building. If you're caught, you're dead. They cut your throat. They rob your apartment and then set fire to it. So: you don't get caught. You move further into Dobrinja. You stay with a friend, maybe a neighbour. But the Chetniks are after you. You go down into the cellar—a mistake?

Now they have you. They keep you there with their shelling: no light, no water, no food. When you can't take it anymore, you go out to pick a dandelion leaf; you want to make salad. You are shot by a sniper: injured, but not killed.

The defenders of Dobrinja catch snipers. They catch the one who shot you. What happens then? The Chetniks ask for the sniper to be delivered and returned to them in exchange for allowing an ambulance to pass to the first hospital, since Dobrinja as well as the rest of Sarajevo is under blockade. So you hand over the Chetnik sniper—the very one who shot and injured you. On the same day, but in another part of town, say at Mojmilo, another Chetnik sniper kills a nurse. So, when you finally reach the hospital, to tend your injury, there is no medicine or food; there is a dead nurse. You are transferred to another hospital, the crowded one, which the Chetniks start shelling from the surrounding hills, after they have eaten roasted pork, drunk brandy and sung their songs. Later, as the ambulance returns—the one that was allowed to pass through the blockade—the Chetniks, let's say from Marshall Tito barracks, kill the driver and steal the vehicle. In the meantime you die in the hospital from the wounds you received from the sniper who was apprehended but returned in exchange for allowing the ambulance to pass, which has now been stolen. They dig you a grave in the nearest park but Chetniks fire at your coffin, at the Muslim priest, at several good and brave men who want to bury you. And when night falls they shell your grave from the mountains.

What do you call this war?

'The wounds are still hurting Haji Tahirović, his torment is unbearable,' I say.

'Yes,' Adem says quietly. 'I know. But the mullah from Vrsinja, his four sons, wife and daughter along with all 176 souls from the burning *masdžid,* are saved.'

'Yes,' I say.

'Yesterday Chetniks near Rogatica burnt down a thousand houses. That is a great number of houses,' Adem Kahriman says.

'There are only five words to light up my mind,' I say. 'The army of Bosnia and Herzegovina.'

DAY NINETEEN OF THE SIEGE OF DOBRINJA. 'I have only read the opening of your book but already many things cannot be seen, in spite of the explanations and the explanation of the explanation.'

'What can't you see?' Adem asks.

'Dobrinja cannot be seen, the apartment blocks, the people, the lawns, the dogs. I can't even number all the things that cannot be seen.' I say.

'This is a book, not a movie,' says Adem. He smiles and adds, 'A book is a book.'

'But the reader hasn't seen those 176 souls of the burnt down *masdžid,*' I persist.

'Would you like to write my book?' asks Adem.

'No, but you can't even see those people coming out of the burning *masdžid*. Can't you show me how these 176 souls are leaving the *masdžid*?'

'They are coming out slowly,' says Adem.

'I see,' I say at last, feeling reconciled. I think and then I say: 'Well, as far as I'm concerned, I will always be able to testify to having seen the *muallim* from Vrsinje, his four sons and daughter sound and alive. That I *have* seen.'

'Thank you,' says Adem.

It is 17 July 1992, the very day Chetniks in the settlement of Vučine near Visegrad push eighty men and women into a cellar of a house and burn them. I don't mention that to Adem Kahriman, although I know that he knows.

When Adem is able to save 183 persons from Dobrinja, why can't I save eighty? I think. But I can't. I can't save them, but neither can Europe—or else it isn't willing to. I can't save them, but neither can America—or else it doesn't want to. I can't, but the whole world can't save them either. Or else it doesn't want to.

Notes on Contributors

Heinrich Böll was awarded the Nobel Prize for Literature in 1972. His novels include *The Lost Honour of Katharina Blum* and *The Clown*; his first novel *Der Engel Schwieg* was recently discovered in the Böll archive in Cologne. He died in 1985. **Hans Magnus Enzensberger** is one of Germany's leading essayists and poets. His books include *Europe, Europe*, a collection of meditations on European cities, and *Mediocrity and Delusion*. **Christa Wolf**'s previous contribution to *Granta*, 'What Remains', appeared in issue 33. **Ian Buruma** is completing a book about the memories of World War Two in Germany and Japan. He lives in London. **Doris Dörrie**'s first collection of short stories, *Love, Pain and the Whole Damn Thing*, was published last year. **Günter Grass**'s 'Losses' was delivered as a lecture on 18 November 1992, five days after German youths fire-bombed a hostel, killing three Turkish women. His most recent novel, *The Call of the Toad*, was published last September. **Monika Maron** was born in Berlin during an Allied bombing attack in 1941. She moved to West Germany in 1988. She is the author of three novels and lives in Hamburg. **Max Thomas Mehr** and **Regine Sylvester** are the deputy editors of *Die Wochenpost*, a Berlin weekly. The East German novelist **Klaus Schlesinger** was expelled from the Writers' Union in 1977; two years later he left the GDR. He now lives in a squat in West Berlin. **Wolf Biermann** was born in Hamburg in 1936, but at the age of seventeen declared his allegiance to the Communist Party and moved to East Germany. In 1976 he was expelled from the Party and the country. His Stasi file is said to be in excess of 30,000 pages. **Russell Hoban**'s collection of stories and essays, *The Moment under the Moment*, was published last year by Jonathan Cape. He is currently at work on an opera with Harrison Birtwhistle. **Pawel Huelle** is a professor in Polish literature at the University of Gdańsk. His first novel, *Who was David Weiser?* won the Independent Foreign Fiction Award in July 1992. **Haruki Murakami** lives in Tokyo. His novel *Dance, Dance, Dance* was published earlier this year. **Martha Gellhorn's** reportage from Germany is included in *The Face of War*, published in a revised form by Granta Books in March. Her peacetime reporting, *The View from the Ground*, is also published by Granta Books. She lives in London and Wales. **Nuha Al-Radi**, the daughter of a diplomat, moved back to Baghdad in 1976. This is her first published work. **Dubravka Ugrešić** teaches literature at the University of Zagreb. She is working on a book of essays about the war in Yugoslavia. **Nedžad Ibrišimović** is a Bosnian writer. As we go to press it is the 157th day of the siege of Dobrinja.